Guy Deverell, v. 2 of 2

by Le Fanu, Joseph Sheridan, 1814-1873

ISBN: 9781318047345

Ordering Information:

Quantity sales. Special discounts are available on quantity purchases by corporations, associations, and others. For details, contact the publisher by email at the address above.

Printed in the United States of America, United Kingdom and Australia

COLLECTION

OF

BRITISH AUTHORS.

VOL. 804.

GUY DEVERELL BY J. S. LE FANU.

IN TWO VOLUMES.

VOL. II.

COLLECTION OF BRITISH AUTHORS.

VOL. 803.

GUY DEVERELL BY J. S. LE FANU.

IN TWO VOLUMES.

VOL. II.

GUY DEVERELL.

BY J. S. LE FANU,

AUTHOR OF "UNCLE SILAS," ETC.

COPYRIGHT EDITION.

IN TWO VOLUMES.

VOL. II.

LEIPZIG BERNHARD TAUCHNITZ

1865.

CONTENTS OF VOLUME II.

GUY DEVERELL.

CHAPTER I.

Lady Alice and Varbarriere tête-à-tête in the Library.

"Well, he told you something, did not he?" persisted Lady Alice.

"In the sense of a distinct disclosure, nothing," said the Bishop, looking demurely over his horizontal leg on the neatly-shorn grass. "He did speak to me upon subjects—his wishes, and I have no doubt he intended to have been much more explicit. In fact, he intimated as much; but he was overtaken by death—unable to speak when I saw him next morning."

"He spoke to you, I know, about pulling down or blowing up that green chamber," said Lady Alice, whose recollections grew a little violent in proportion to the Bishop's reserve and her own impatience.

"He did not suggest quite such strong measures, but he did regret that it had ever been built, and made me promise to urge upon his son, as you once before mentioned you were aware, so soon as he should come of age, to shut it up."

"And you did urge him?"

"Certainly, Lady Alice," said the Bishop, with dignity. "I viewed it in the light of a duty, and a very sacred one, to do so."

"He told you the reason, then?" inquired Lady Alice.

"He gave me no reason on earth for his wish; perhaps, had he been spared for another day, he would have done so; but he expressed himself strongly indeed, with a kind of horror, and spoke of the Italian who built, and his father who ordered it, in terms of strong disapprobation, and wished frequently it had never been erected. Perhaps you would like to take a little turn. How very pretty the flowers still are!"

"Very. No, thank you, I'll sit a little. And there was something more. I know perfectly there was, my lord; what was it, pray?" answered the old lady.

"It was merely something that I took charge of," said the Bishop, cautiously.

"You need not be so reserved with me, my lord; I'm not, as you very well know, a talking old woman, by any means. I know something of the matter already, and have never talked about it; and as the late Lady Marlowe was my poor daughter by marriage, you may talk to me, I should hope, a little more freely than to a total stranger."

The Bishop, I fancy, thought there was something in this appeal, and was, perhaps, amused at the persistency of women, for he smiled sadly for a second or two on his gaiter, and he said, looking before him with his head a little on one side—

"You give me credit, my dear Lady Alice, for a great deal more reserve than I have, at least on this occasion, exercised. I have very little to disclose, and I am not forbidden by any promise, implied or direct, to tell you the very little I know."

He paused.

"Well, my lord, *pray* go on," insisted Lady Alice.

"Yes, on the whole," said the Bishop, thoughtfully, "I prefer telling you. In the room in which he died, in this house, there is, or was, a sort of lock-up place."

"That was the room in which Jekyl now sleeps," interrupted Lady Alice.

"I am not aware."

"The room at the extreme back of the house. You go through a long passage on the same level as the hall, and then, at the head of the far back-stair, into a small room on your left, and through that into the bed-room, I mean. It was there, I know, his coffin lay, for I saw him in it."

"As well as I recollect, that must have been the room. I know it lay as you describe. He gave me some keys that were placed with his purse under his pillow, and directed me to open the press, and take out a box, resembling a small oak plate-chest, which I did, and, by his direction, having unlocked it, I took out a very little trunk-shaped box, covered with stamped red leather, and he took it from me, and the keys, and that time said no more."

"Well?"

"In the evening, when I returned, he said he had been thinking about it, and wished to place it and the key in my care, as his boy was not of age, and it contained something, the value of which, as I understood, might be overlooked, and the box mislaid. His direction to me was to give it to his son, the present Sir Jekyl, on his coming of age, and to tell him from him that he was to do what was right with it. I know those were his words, for he was exhausted, and not speaking very distinctly; and I repeated them carefully after him, and as he said, 'correctly;' after a short time he added, 'I think I shall tell you more about it to-morrow;' but, as I told you, he was unable to speak next morning."

"And what did that red box contain?" asked Lady Alice.

"I can't tell. I never unlocked it. I tied it round with a tape and sealed it, and so it remained."

"Then, Jekyl got it when he came of age?"

"I had him, about that time, at my house. He examined the box, and, when he had satisfied himself as to its contents, he secured it again with his own seal, and requested me to keep it for him for some short time longer."

"Have you got it still in your possession?"

"No. I thought it best to insist at last on his taking it into his own keeping. I've brought it with me here—and I gave it to him on the day of my arrival."

"Very heavy, was it?"

"On the contrary, very light."

"H'm! Thank you, my lord; it is very good of you to converse so long with an old woman such as I."

"On the contrary, Lady Alice, I am much obliged to you. The fact is, I believe it is better to have mentioned these circumstances. It may, perhaps, prove important that some member of the family should know exactly what took place between me and the late Sir Harry Marlowe during his last illness. You now know everything. I have reminded him, as I thought it right, of the earnest injunction of his father, first with respect to that room, the green chamber; and he tells me that he means to comply with it when his party shall have broken up. And about the other matter, the small box, I mentioned that he should do what is right with it. He asked me if I had seen what the box contained; and on my saying no, he added that he could not tell what his father meant by telling him to do what was right with it—in fact, that he could do nothing with it."

"Quite an Italian evening!" exclaimed the Bishop, after a pause, rising, and offering his arm to Lady Alice.

And so their conference ended.

Next day, contrary to her secluded custom, and for the first time, Lady Alice glided feebly into the new library of Marlowe, of which all the guests were free.

Quite empty, except of that silent company in Russia leather and gold, in vellum, and other fine suits; all so unobtrusive and quiet; all so obsequiously at her service; all ready to speak their best, their brightest, and wisest thoughts, or to be silent and neglected, and yet never affronted; always alert to serve and speak, or lie quiet.

Quite deserted! No, not quite. There, more than half hidden by that projection and carved oak pilaster, sate Monsieur Varbarriere, in an easy-chair and a pair of gold spectacles, reading easily his vellum quarto.

"Pretty room!" exclaimed Lady Alice in soliloquy, so soon as she had detected the corpulent and grave student.

Monsieur Varbarriere laid down his book with a look of weariness, and seeing Lady Alice, smiled benignly, and rose and bowed, and his sonorous bass tones greeted her courteously from the nook in which he stood framed in oak, like a portrait of a rich and mysterious burgomaster.

"What a pretty room!" repeated the old lady; "I believe we are *tête-à-tête*."

"Quite so; I have been totally alone; a most agreeable surprise, Lady Alice. Books are very good company; but even the best won't do always; and I was beginning to weary of mine."

M. Varbarriere spoke French, so did Lady Alice; in fact, for that gentleman's convenience, all conversations with him in that house were conducted in the same courtly language.

Lady Alice looked round the room to satisfy herself that they were really alone; and having made her commendatory criticisms on the apartment once more,

"Very pretty," echoed Monsieur Varbarriere; "I admire the oak, especially in a library, it is so solemn and contemplative. The Bishop was here to-day, and admired the room very much. An agreeable and good man the Bishop appears to be."

"Yes; a good man; an excellent man. I had a very interesting conversation with him yesterday. I may as well tell you, Monsieur Varbarriere—I know I may rely upon you—I have not come to my time of life without knowing pretty well, by a kind of instinct, whom

I may trust; and I well know how you sympathise with me about my lost son."

"Profoundly, madame;" and Monsieur Varbarriere, with his broad and brown hand on his breast, bowed slowly and very deep.

CHAPTER II.

M. Varbarriere orders his Wings.

In her own way, with interjections, and commentary and occasional pauses for the sake of respiration, old Lady Alice related the substance of what the Bishop had communicated to her.

"And what do you suppose, Monsieur Varbarriere, to have been the contents of that red leather box?" asked Lady Alice.

Monsieur Varbarriere smiled mysteriously and nodded.

"I fancy, Lady Alice, I have the honour to have arrived at precisely the same conclusion with yourself," said he.

"Well, I dare say. You see now what is involved. You understand now why I should be, for his own sake, more than ever grieved that my boy is gone," she said, trembling very much.

Monsieur Varbarriere bowed profoundly.

"And why it is, sir, that I do insist on your explaining your broken phrase of the other evening."

Monsieur Varbarriere in his deep oak frame stood up tall, portly, and erect. A narrow window, with stained heraldic emblazonry, was partly behind him, and the light from above fell askance on one side of his massive countenance, throwing such dark downward bars of shadow on his face, that Lady Alice could not tell whether he was scowling or smiling, or whether the effect was an illusion.

"What phrase, pray, does your ladyship allude to?" he inquired.

"You spoke of my boy—my poor Guy—as if you knew more of him than you cared to speak—as if you were on the point of disclosing, and suddenly recollected yourself," replied Lady Alice.

"You mean when I had the honour to converse with you the night before last in the drawing-room," said he, a little brusquely, observing that the old lady was becoming vehemently excited.

"Yes; when you left me under the impression that you thought my son still living," half screamed Lady Alice, like a woman in a fury.

"Bah!" thundered the sneering diapason of Monsieur Varbarriere, whose good manners totally forsook him in his angry impatience, and his broad foot on the floor enforced his emphasis with a stamp.

"What do you mean, you foreign masquerader, whom nobody knows? What *can* it be? Sir, you have half distracted me. I've heard of people getting into houses—I've heard of magicians—I've heard of the devil—I have heard of charlatans, sir. I'd like to know what right, if you know nothing of my dear son, you have to torture me with doubts—"

"Doubts!" repeated Varbarriere, if less angrily, even more contemptuously. "Pish!"

"You may say *pish*, sir, or any rudeness you please; but depend upon this, if you do know *anything* of any kind, about my darling son, I'll have it from you if there be either laws or men in England," shrieked Lady Alice.

Varbarriere all at once subsided, and looked hesitatingly. In tones comparatively quiet, but still a little ruffled, he said—

"I've been, I fear, very rude; everyone that's angry is. I think you are right. I ought never to have approached the subject of your domestic sorrow. It was not my doing, madame; it was *you* who insisted on drawing me to it."

"You told me that you had seen my son, and knew Mr. Strangways intimately."

"I did *not!*" cried Varbarriere sternly, with his head thrown back; and he and Lady Alice for a second or two were silent. "That is, I beg pardon, you *misapprehended* me. I'm sure I never could have said I had seen your son, Mr. Guy Deverell, or that I had a particularly intimate acquaintance with Mr. Strangways."

"It won't do," burst forth Lady Alice again; "I'll not be fooled—I won't be fooled, sir."

"Pray, then, pause for one moment before you have excited an alarm in the house, and possibly decide me on taking my leave for ever," said Varbarriere, in a low but very stern tone. "Whatever I may be—charlatan, conjurer, devil—if you but knew the truth, you would acknowledge yourself profoundly and everlastingly indebted to me. It *is* quite true that I am in possession of facts of which you had not even a suspicion; it is true that the affairs of those nearest to you in blood have occupied my profoundest thoughts and most affectionate care. I believe, if you will but exercise the self-command of which I have no doubt you are perfectly capable, for a very few days, I shall have so matured my plans as to render their defeat impracticable. On the other hand, if you give me any trouble, or induce the slightest suspicion anywhere that I have taken an interest of the kind I describe, I shall quit England, and you shall go down to your grave in *darkness*, and with the conviction, moreover, that you have blasted the hopes for which you ought to have sacrificed not your momentary curiosity only, but your unhappy life."

Lady Alice was awed by the countenance and tones of this strange man, who assumed an authority over her, on this occasion, which neither of her deceased lords had ever ventured to assert in their lifetimes.

Her fearless spirit would not, however, succumb, but looked out through the cold windows of her deep-set eyes into the fiery gaze of her *master*, as she felt him, daringly as before.

After a short pause, she said—

"You would have acted more wisely, Monsieur Varbarriere, had you spoken to me on other occasions as frankly as you have just now done."

"Possibly, madame."

"Certainly, monsieur."

M. Varbarriere bowed.

"Certainly, sir. But having at length heard so much, I am willing to concede what you say. I trust the delay may not be long.—I think you ought to tell me soon. I suppose we had better talk no more in the interim," she added, suddenly turning as she approached the threshold of the room, and recovering something of her lofty tone— "upon that, to me, terrible subject."

"*Much* better, madame," acquiesced M. Varbarriere.

"And we meet otherwise as before," said the old lady, with a disdainful condescension and a slight bow.

"I thank you, madame, for that favour," replied M. Varbarriere, reverentially, approaching the door, which, as she drew near to withdraw, he opened for her with a bow, and they parted.

"I hope she'll be quiet, that old grey wildcat. I must get a note from her to Madame Gwynn. The case grows stronger; a little more and it will be irresistible, if only that stupid and ill-tempered old woman can be got to govern herself for a few days."

That evening, in the drawing-room, Monsieur Varbarriere was many degrees more respectful than ever to that old grey wildcat, at whom that morning he had roared in a way so utterly ungentlemanlike and ferocious.

People at a distance might have almost fancied a sexagenarian caricature of a love-scene. There had plainly been the lovers' quarrel. The lady carried her head a little high, threw sidelong glances on the carpet, had a little pink flush in her cheeks, and spoke little; listened, but smiled not; while the gentleman sat as close as he dare, and spoke earnestly and low.

Monsieur Varbarriere was, in fact, making the most of his time, and recovering all he could of his milder influence over Lady Alice, and did persuade and soften; and at length he secured a promise of the note he wanted to Mrs. Gwynn, pledging his honour that she would thoroughly approve the object of it, so soon as he was at liberty to disclose it.

That night, taking leave of Sir Jekyl, Monsieur Varbarriere said—

"You've been so good as to wish me to prolong my visit, which has been to me so charming and so interesting. I have ventured, therefore, to enable myself to do so, by arranging an absence of two days, which I mean to devote to business which will not bear postponement."

"Very sorry to lose you, even for the time you say; but you must leave your nephew, Mr. Strangways, as a hostage in our hands to secure your return."

"He shall remain, as you are so good as to desire it, to enjoy himself. As for me, I need no tie to hold me to my engagement, and only regret every minute stolen for other objects from my visit."

There was some truth in these complimentary speeches. Sir Jekyl was now quite at ease as to the character of his guests, whom he had at first connected with an often threatened attack, which he profoundly dreaded, however lightly he might talk of its chances of success. The host, on the whole, liked his guests, and really wished their stay prolonged; and Monsieur Varbarriere, who silently observed many things of which he did not speak, was, perhaps, just now particularly interested in his private perusal of that little romance which was to be read only at Marlowe Manor.

"I see, Guy, you have turned over a new leaf—no fooling now—you must not relapse, mind. I shall be away for two days. If longer, address me at Slowton. May I rely on your good sense and resolution—knowing what are our probable relations with this family—to continue to exercise the same caution as I have observed in your conduct, with much satisfaction, for the last two evenings? Well, I suppose I may. If you cannot trust yourself—fly. Get away—pack. You may follow me to Slowton, make what excuse you please; but don't loiter here. Good-night."

Such was the farewell spoken by Varbarriere to his nephew, as he nodded his good-night on the threshold of their dressing-room.

In the morning Monsieur Varbarriere's place knew him no more at the breakfast-table. With his valise, despatch-box, and desk, he had glided away, in the frosty sunlight, in a Marlowe post-chaise, to the "Plough Inn," on the Old London Road, where, as we know, he had once sojourned before. It made a slight roundabout to the point to which his business really invited his route; and as he dismissed his vehicle here, I presume it was done with a view to mystify possible inquirers.

At the "Plough Inn" he was received with an awful bustle and reverence. The fame of the consideration with which he was entertained at Marlowe had reached that modest hostelry, and Monsieur Varbarriere looked larger, grander, more solemn in its modest hall, than ever; his valise was handled with respect, and lifted in like an invalid, not hauled and trundled like a prisoner; and the desk and despatch-box, as the more immediate attendants on his person, were eyed with the respect which such a confidence could not fail to inspire.

So Monsieur Varbarriere, having had his appetising drive through a bright country and keen air, ate his breakfast very comfortably; and when that meal was over, ordered a "fly," in which he proceeded to Wardlock, and pulled up at the hall-door of Lady Alice's reserved-looking, but comfortable old redbrick mansion.

CHAPTER III.

Monsieur Varbarriere talks with Donica Gwynn.

The footman opened the door in deshabille and unshorn, with a countenance that implied his sense of the impertinence of this disturbance of his gentlemanlike retirement. There was, however, that in the countenance of Monsieur Varbarriere, as well as the intangible but potent "aura" emitted by wealth, which surrounded him—an influence which everybody feels and no one can well define, which circumambiates a rich person and makes it felt, nobody knows how, that he *is* wealthy—that brought the flunky to himself; and adjusting his soiled necktie hastily with one hand, he ran down to the heavy but commanding countenance that loomed on his from the window of the vehicle.

"This is Wardlock?" demanded the visitor.

"Wardlock Manor?—yes, sir," answered the servant.

"I've a note from Lady Alice Redcliffe, and a few words to Mrs. Gwynn the housekeeper. She's at home?"

"Mrs. Gwynn?—yes, sir."

"Open the door, please," said Monsieur Varbarriere, who was now speaking good frank English with wonderful fluency, considering his marked preference for the French tongue elsewhere.

The door flew open at the touch of the footman; and Monsieur Varbarriere entered the staid mansion, and was shown by the servant into the wainscoted parlour in which Lady Alice had taken leave of the ancient retainer whom he was about to confer with.

When Mrs. Gwynn, with that mixture of curiosity and apprehension which an unexpected visit is calculated to inspire, entered the room, very erect and natty, she saw a large round-shouldered stranger, standing with his back toward her, arrayed in black, at the window, with his grotesque high-crowned hat on.

Turning about he removed this with a slight bow and a grave smile, and with his sonorous foreign accent inquired—

"Mrs. Gwynn, I suppose?"

"Yes, sir, that is my name, if you please."

"A note, Mrs. Gwynn, from Lady Alice Redcliffe."

And as he placed it in the thin and rather ladylike fingers of the housekeeper, his eyes rested steadily on her features, as might those of a process-server, whose business it might be hereafter to identify her.

Mrs. Gwynn read the note, which was simply an expression of her mistress's wish that she should answer explicitly whatever questions the gentleman, M. Varbarriere, who would hand it to her, and who was, moreover, a warm friend of the family, might put to her.

When Mrs. Gwynn, with the help of her spectacles, had spelled through this letter, she in turn looked searchingly at Monsieur Varbarriere, and began to wonder unpleasantly what line his examination might take.

"Will you, Mrs. Gwynn, allow me the right to sit down, by yourself taking a chair?" said Monsieur Varbarriere, very politely, smiling darkly, and waving his hand toward a seat.

"I'm very well as I am, I thank you, sir," replied Gwynn, who did not very much like the gentleman's looks, and thought him rather like a great roguish Jew pedlar whom she had seen long ago at the fair of Marlowe.

"Nay, but pray sit down—I can't while you stand—and our conversation may last some time—pray do."

"I can talk as well, sir, one way as t'other," replied she, while at the same time, with a sort of fidgeted impatience, she did sit down and fold her hands in her lap.

"We have all, Mrs. Gwynn, a very high opinion of you; I mean Lady Alice and the friends of her family, among whom I reckon myself."

"It's only of late as I came to my present misses, you're aware, sir, 'aving been, from, I may say, my childhood in the Marlowe family."

"I know—the Marlowe family—it's all one, in fact; but I may say, Mrs. Gwynn, that short, comparatively, as has been your time with Lady Alice, you are spoken of with more respect and liking by that branch of the family than by Sir Jekyl."

"I've done nothing to disoblege Sir Jekyl, as Lady Alice knows. Will you be so kind, sir, as to say what you want of me, having business to attend to up-stairs?"

"Certainly, it is only a trifle or two."

Monsieur Varbarriere cleared his voice.

"Having ascertained all about that *secret door* that opens into the green chamber at Marlowe, we would be obliged to you to let us know at what time, to your knowledge, it was first used."

His large full eyes, from under his projecting brows, stared full upon her shrinking gaze as he asked this question in tones deep and firm, but otherwise as civil as he could employ.

It was vain for Mrs. Gwynn to attempt to conceal her extreme agitation. Her countenance showed it—she tried to speak, and failed; and cleared her throat, and broke down again.

"Perhaps you'd like some water," said Varbarriere, rising and approaching the bell.

"No," said Donica Gwynn, rising suddenly and getting before him. "Let be."

He saw that she wished to escape observation.

"As you please, Mrs. Gwynn—sit down again—I shan't without your leave—and recover a little."

"There's nothing wrong with me, sir," replied Donica, now in possession of her voice, very angrily; "there's nothing to cause it."

"Well, Mrs. Gwynn, it's quite excusable; I know all about it."

"What *are* you, a builder or a hartist?"

"Nothing of the kind; I'm a gentleman without a profession, Mrs. Gwynn, and one who will not permit you to be compromised; one who will protect you from the slightest suspicion of anything unpleasant."

"I don't know what you're a-driving at," said Mrs. Gwynn, still as white as death, and glancing furiously.

"Come, Mrs. Gwynn, you're a sensible woman. You *do* know *perfectly*. You have maintained a respectable character."

"Yes, sir!" said Donica Gwynn, and suddenly burst into a paroxysm of hysterical tears.

"Listen to me: you have maintained a respectable character, I know it: nothing whatever to injure that character shall ever fall from my lips; no human being—but two or three just as much interested in concealing all about it as you or I—shall ever know anything about it; and Sir Jekyl Marlowe has consented to take it down, so soon as the party at present at Marlowe shall have dispersed."

"Lady Alice—I'll never like to see her again," sobbed Donica.

"Lady Alice has no more suspicion of the existence of that door than the Pope of Rome has; and what is more, never shall. You may rely upon me to observe the most absolute silence and secrecy—nay, more, if necessary for the object of concealment—so to mislead and mystify people, that they can never so much as surmise the truth, *provided*—pray observe me—*provided* you treat me with the most *absolute candour*. You must not practise the least reserve or concealment. On tracing the slightest shadow of either in your communication with me, I hold myself free to deal with the facts in my possession, precisely as may seem best to myself. You understand?"

"Not Lady Alice, nor none of the servants, nor—nor a creature living, please."

"*Depend* on me," said Varbarriere.

"Well, sure I may; a gentleman would not break his word with such as me," said Donica, imploringly.

"We can't spend the whole day repeating the same thing over and over," said Varbarriere, rather grimly; "I've said my say—I know everything that concerns *you* about it, without your opening your lips upon the subject. You occupied that room for two years and a half during Sir Harry's lifetime—you see I know it all. *There!* you are perfectly safe. I need not have made you any promise, but I do—perfectly safe with me—and the room shall vanish this winter, and no one but ourselves know anything of that door—do you understand?—*provided*—"

"Yes, sir, please—and what do you wish to know more from me? I don't know, I'm sure, why I should be such a fool as to take on so about it, as if *I* could help it, or was ever a bit the worse of it myself. There's been many a one has slep' in that room and never so much as knowd there was a door but that they came in by."

"To be sure; so tell me, do you recollect Mr. Deverell's losing a paper in that room?"

"Well, I do mind the time he said he lost it there, but I know no more than the child unborn."

"Did Sir Harry never tell you?"

"They said a deal o' bad o' Sir Harry, and them that should a' stood up for him never said a good word for him. Poor old creature!—I doubt if he had pluck to do it. I don't think he had, poor fellow!"

"Did he ever *tell* you he had done it? Come, remember your promise."

"No, upon my soul—never."

"Do you *think* he took it?"

Their eyes met steadily.

"Yes, I do," said she, with a slight defiant frown.

"And *why* do you think so?"

"Because, shortly after the row began about that paper, he talked with me, and said there was something a-troubling of him, and he wished me to go and live in a farm-house at Applehythe, and keep summat he wanted kep safe, as there was no one in all England so true as me—poor old fellow! He never told me, and I never asked. But I laid it down in my own mind it was the paper Mr. Deverell lost, that's all."

"Did he ever show you that paper?"

"No."

"Did he tell you where it was?"

"He never said he had it."

"Did he show you where that thing was which he wanted you to take charge of?"

"Yes, in the press nigh his bed's head."

"Did he open the press?"

"Ay."

"Well?"

"He showed me a sort of a box, and he said that was all."

"A little trunk of stamped red leather—was that like it?"

"That was just it."

"Did he afterwards give it into anybody's charge?"

"I know no more about it. I saw it there, that's all. I saw it once, and never before nor since."

"Is there more than one secret door into that room?" pursued Varbarriere.

"More than one; no, never as I heard or thought."

"Where is the door placed with which *you* are acquainted?"

"Why? Don't you know?"

"Suppose I know of two. We have discovered a second. Which is the one you saw used? *Come!*"

Parenthetically it is to be observed that no such discovery had been made, and Varbarriere was merely fishing for information without disclosing his ignorance.

"In the recess at the right of the bed's head."

"Yes; and how do you open it? I mean from the green chamber?"

"I never knowd any way how to open it—it's from t'other side. There's a way to bolt it, though."

"Ay? How's that?"

"There's an ornament of scrowl-work, they calls it, bronze-like, as runs down the casing of the recess, shaped like letter esses. Well, the fourteenth of them, reckoning up from the bottom, next the wall, turns round with your finger and thumb; so if anyone be in the green chamber, and knows the secret, they can stop the door being opened."

"I see—thank you. You've been through the passage leading from Sir Harry's room that was—Sir Jekyl Marlowe's room, at the back of the house, to the secret door of the green chamber?"

"No, never. I know nothink o' that, no more nor a child."

"No?"

"No, nothink at all."

Varbarriere had here been trying to establish another conjecture.

There was a pause. Varbarriere, ruminating darkly, looked on Donica Gwynn. He then closed his pocket-book, in which he had inscribed a few notes, and said—

"Thank you, Mrs. Gwynn. Should I want anything more I'll call again; and you had better not mention the subject of my visit. Let me see the pictures—that will be the excuse—and do *you* keep *your* secret, and I'll keep mine."

"No, I thank you, sir," said Donica, drily, almost fiercely, drawing back from his proffered douceur.

"Tut, tut—pray do."

"No, I thank you."

So he looked at the pictures in the different rooms, and at some old china and snuff-boxes, to give a colour to his visit; and with polite speeches and dark smiles, and a general courtesy that was unctuous, he took his leave of Donica Gwynn, whom he left standing in the hall with a flushed face and a sore heart.

CHAPTER IV.

A Story of a Magician and a Vampire.

The pleasant autumn sun touched the steep roofs and mullioned windows of Marlowe Manor pleasantly that morning, turning the thinning foliage of its noble timber into gold, and bringing all the slopes and undulations of its grounds into relief in its subdued glory. The influence of the weather was felt by the guests assembled in the spacious breakfast-parlour, and gay and animated was the conversation.

Lady Jane Lennox, that "superbly handsome creature," as old Doocey used to term her, had relapsed very much into her old ways. Beatrix had been pleased when, even in her impetuous and uncertain way, that proud spirit had seemed to be drawn toward her again. But that was past, and that unruly nature had broken away once more upon her own solitary and wayward courses. She cared no more for Beatrix, or, if at all, it was plainly not kindly.

In Lady Jane's bold and mournful isolation there was something that interested Beatrix, ungracious as her ways often were, and she felt sore at the unjust repulse she had experienced. But Beatrix was proud, and so, though wounded, she did not show her pain—not that pain, nor another far deeper.

Between her and Guy Strangways had come a coldness unintelligible to her, an estrangement which she would have felt like an insult, had it not been for his melancholy looks and evident loss of spirits.

There is a very pretty room at Marlowe; it is called (*why*, I forget) Lady Mary's boudoir; its door opens from the first landing on the great stair. An oak floor, partly covered with a Turkey carpet, one tall window with stone shafts, a high old-fashioned stone chimneypiece, and furniture perhaps a little incongruous, but pleasant in its incongruity. Tapestry in the Teniers style—Dutch village festivals, with no end of figures, about half life-size, dancing, drinking, making music; old boors, and young and fair-haired maidens, and wrinkled vraus, and here and there gentlemen in doublets and plumed hats, and ladies, smiling and bare-headed, and fair and plump, in great stomachers. These pleasant subjects, so lifelike, with children, cocks and hens, and dogs interspersed, helped, with a Louis Quatorze suit of pale green, and gold chairs cushioned with Utrecht velvet, to give to this room its character so mixed, of gaiety and solemnity, something very quaint and cheery.

This room had old Lady Alice Redcliffe selected for her sitting-room, when she found herself unequal to the exertion of meeting the other ladies in the drawing-room, and hither she had been wont to invite Guy Strangways, who would occasionally pass an hour here wonderfully pleasantly and happily—in fact, as many hours as the old lady would have permitted, so long as Beatrix had been her companion.

But with those self-denying resolutions we have mentioned came a change. When Beatrix was there the young gentleman was grave and rather silent, and generally had other engagements which at least shortened his visit. This was retorted by Beatrix, who, a few minutes after the arrival of the visitor whom old Lady Alice had begun to call her secretary, would, on one pretence or another, disappear, and leave the old princess and her secretary to the uninterrupted enjoyment of each other's society.

Now since the night on which Varbarriere in talking with Lady Alice had, as we have heard, suddenly arrested his speech respecting her son—leaving her in uncertainty how it was to have been finished—an uncertainty on which her morbid brain reflected a thousand horrid and impossible shapes, the old lady had once more conceived something of her early dread of Guy Strangways. It was now again subsiding, although last night, under the influence of laudanum, in her medicated sleep her son had been sitting at her bedside, talking incessantly, she could not remember what.

Guy Strangways had just returned from the Park for his fishing-rod and angler's gear, when he was met in the hall by the grave and courteous butler, who presented a tiny pencilled note from Lady Alice, begging him to spare her half an hour in Lady Mary's boudoir.

Perhaps it was a bore. But habitual courtesy is something more than "mouth honour, breath." Language and thought react upon one another marvellously. To restrain its expression is in part to restrain the feeling; and thus a well-bred man is not only in words and demeanour, but inwardly and sincerely, more gracious and noble than others.

How oddly things happen sometimes!

Exactly as Guy Strangways arrived on the lobby, a little gloved hand—it was Beatrix's—was on the door-handle of Lady Mary's boudoir. It was withdrawn, and she stood looking for a second or two at the young gentleman, who had evidently been going in the same direction. He, too, paused; then, with a very low bow, advanced to open the door for Miss Marlowe.

"No, thank you—I—I think I had better postpone my visit to grandmamma till I return. I'm going to the garden, and should like to bring her some flowers."

"I'm afraid I have arrived unluckily—she would, I know, have been so glad to see you," said Guy Strangways.

"Oh, I've seen her twice before to-day. You were going to make her a little visit now."

"I—if you wish it, Miss Marlowe, I'll defer it."

"She would be very little obliged to me, I'm sure; but I must really go," said Beatrix, recollecting on a sudden that there was no need of so long a parley.

"It would very much relieve the poor secretary's labours, and make his little period of duty so much happier," said Guy, forgetting his wise resolutions strangely.

"I am sure grandmamma would prefer seeing her visitors singly—it makes a great deal more of them, you know."

And with a little smile and such a pretty glow in her cheeks, she passed him by. He bowed and smiled faintly too, and for a moment stood gazing after her into the now vacant shadow of the old oak wainscoting, as young Numa might after his vanished Egeria, with an unspoken, burning grief and a longing at his heart.

"I'm sure she can't like me—I'm sure she *dis*likes me. So much the better—Heaven knows I'm glad of it."

And with an aching heart he knocked, turned the handle, and entered the pretty apartment in which Lady Alice, her thin shoulders curved, as she held her hands over the fire, was sitting alone.

She looked at him over her shoulder strangely from her hollow eyes, without moving or speaking for a time. He bowed gravely, and said—

"I have this moment received your little note, Lady Alice, and have hastened to obey."

She sat up straight and sighed.

"Thanks—I have not been very well—so nervous—so very nervous," she repeated, without removing her sad and clouded gaze from his face.

"We all heard with regret that you had not been so well," said he.

"Well, we'll not talk of it—you're very good—I'm glad you've come—very nervous, and almost wishing myself back at Wardlock—where indeed I should have returned, only that I should have been wishing myself back again before an hour—miserably nervous."

And Lady Alice sniffed at her smelling-salts, and added—

"And Monsieur Varbarriere gone away on business for some days—is not he?"

"Yes—quite uncertain—possibly for two, or perhaps three, he said," answered Guy.

"And he's very—he knows—he knows a great deal—I forget what I was going to say—I'm half asleep to-day—no sleep—a very bad night."

And old Lady Alice yawned drearily into the fire.

"Beatrix said she'd look in; but everyone forgets—you young people are so selfish."

"Mademoiselle Marlowe was at the door as I came in, and said she would go on instead to the garden first, and gather some flowers for you."

"Oh! h'm!—very good—well, I can't talk to-day; suppose you choose a book, Mr. Strangways, and read a few pages—that is, if you are quite at leisure?"

"Perfectly—that is, for an hour—unfortunately I have then an appointment. What kind of book shall I take?" he asked, approaching one of the two tall bookstands that flanked an oval mirror opposite the fireplace.

"Anything, provided it is old."

Nearly half an hour passed in discussing what to read—the old lady not being in the mood that day to pursue the verse readings which had employed Guy Strangways hitherto.

"This seems a curious old book," he said, after a few minutes. "Very old French—I think upon witchcraft, and full of odd narratives."

"That will do very well."

"I had better try to translate it—the language is so antiquated."

He leaned the folio on the edge of the chimneypiece, and his elbow beside it, supporting his head on his hand, and so read aloud to the *exigeante* old lady, who liked to see people employed about her, even though little of comfort, amusement, or edification resulted from it.

The narrative which Lady Alice had selected was entitled thus:—

"CONCERNING A REMARKABLE REVENGE AFTER SEPULTURE.

"In the Province of Normandy, in the year of grace 1405, there lived a young gentleman of Styrian descent, possessing estates in Hungary, but a still more opulent fortune in France. His park abutted on that of the Chevalier de St. Aubrache, who was a man also young, of ancient lineage, proud to excess, and though wealthy, by no means so wealthy as his Styrian neighbour.

"This disparity in riches excited the wrath of the jealous nobleman, who having once admitted the passions of envy and hatred to his heart, omitted no opportunity to injure him.

"The Chevalier de St. Aubrache, in fact, succeeded so well—"

Just at this point in the tale, Beatrix, with her flowers, not expecting to find Guy Strangways still in attendance, entered the room.

"You need not go; come in, dear—you've brought me some flowers—come in, I say; thank you, Beatrix, dear—they are very pretty, and very sweet too. Here is Mr. Strangways—sit by me, dear—reading a curious old tale of witchcraft. Tell her the beginning, pray."

So Strangways told the story over again in his best way, and then proceeded to read as follows:—

"The Chevalier de St. Aubrache, in fact, succeeded so well, that on a point of law, aided by a corrupt judge in the Parliament of Rouen, he took from him a considerable portion of his estate, and subsequently so managed matters without committing himself, that he lost his life unfairly in a duel, which the Chevalier secretly contrived.

"Now there was in the household of the gentleman so made away with, a certain Hungarian, older than he, a grave and politic man, and reputed to have studied the art of magic deeply. By this man was the corpse of the deceased gentleman duly coffined, had away to Styria, and, it is said, there buried according to certain conditions, with which the Hungarian magician, who had vowed a terrible revenge, was well acquainted.

"In the meantime the Chevalier de St. Aubrache had espoused a very beautiful demoiselle of the noble family of D'Ayenterre, by whom he had one daughter, so beautiful that she was the subject of universal admiration, which increased in the heart of her proud father that affection which it was only natural that he should cherish for her.

"It was about the time of Candlemas, a full score of years after the death of his master, that the Hungarian magician returned to Normandy, accompanied by a young gentleman, very pale indeed, but otherwise so exactly like the gentleman now so long dead, that no one who had been familiar with his features could avoid being struck, and indeed, affrighted with the likeness.

"The Chevalier de St. Aubrache was at first filled with horror, like the rest; but well knowing that the young man whom he, the stranger, so resembled, had been actually killed as aforesaid, in combat, and having never heard of vampires, which are among the most malignant and awful of the manifestations of the Evil One, and not recognising at all the Hungarian magician, who had been careful to disguise himself effectually; and, above all, relying on letters from the King of Hungary, with which, under a feigned name, as well as with others from the Archbishop of Toledo in Spain, he had come provided, he received him into his house; when the grave magician, who resembled a doctor of a university, and the fair-seeming vampire, being established in the house of their enemy, began to practise, by stealth, their infernal arts."

The old lady saw that in the reader's countenance, as he read this odd story, which riveted her gaze. Perhaps conscious of her steady and uncomfortable stare, as well as of a real parallel, he grew obviously disconcerted, and at last, as it seemed, even agitated as he proceeded.

"Young man, for Heaven's sake, will you tell me who you are?" said Lady Alice, her dark old eyes fixed fearfully on his face, as she rose unconsciously from her chair.

The young man, very pale, turned a despairing and almost savage look from her to Beatrix, and back to her again.

"You are not a Strangways," she continued.

He looked steadily at her, as if he were going to speak, then dropped his glance suddenly and remained silent.

"I say, I know your name is not Strangways," said the old lady, in increasing agitation.

"I can tell you nothing about myself," said he again, fixing his great dark eyes, that looked almost wild in his pallid face, full upon her, with a strange expression of anguish.

"In the Almighty's name, are you Guy Deverell?" she screamed, lifting up her thin hands between him and her in her terror.

The young man returned her gaze oddly, with, she fancied, a look of baffled horror in his face. It seemed to her like an evil spirit detected.

He recovered, however, for a few seconds, something of his usual manner. Instead of speaking, he bowed twice very low, and, on the point of leaving the room, he suddenly arrested his departure, turning about with a stamp on the floor; and walking back to her, he said, very gently—

"Yes, yes, why should I deny it? My name *is* Guy Deverell."

And was gone.

CHAPTER V.

Farewell.

"Oh! grandmamma, *what* is it?" said Beatrix, clasping her thin wrist.

The old lady, stooping over the chair on which she leaned, stared darkly after the vanished image, trembling very much.

"*What* is Deverell—why should the name be so dreadful—is there anything—oh! grandmamma, *is* there anything very bad?"

"I don't know—I am confused—did you ever see such a face? My gracious Heaven!" muttered Lady Alice.

"Oh! grandmamma, darling, tell me what it is, I implore of you."

"Yes, dear, everything; another time. I can't now. I might do a mischief. I might prevent—you must promise me, darling, to tell no one. You must not say his name is Deverell. *You* say nothing about it. That dreadful, dreadful story!"

The folio was lying with crumpled leaves, back upward, on the floor, where it had fallen.

"There is something plainly fearful in it. *You* think so, grandmamma; something discovered; something going to happen. Send after him, grandmamma; call him back. If it is anything you can prevent, I'll ring."

"Don't *touch* the bell," cried granny, sharply, clutching at her hand, "don't *do* it. See, Beatrix, you promise me you say nothing to anyone of what you've witnessed—*promise*. I'll tell you all I know when I'm better. He'll come again. I *wish* he'd come again. I'm sure he will, though I hardly think I could bear to see him. I don't know what to think."

The old lady threw herself back in her chair, not affectedly at all, but looking so awfully haggard and agitated that Beatrix was frightened.

"Call nobody, there's a darling; just open the window; I shall be better."

And she heaved some of those long and heavy sighs which relieve hysterical oppression; and, after a long silence, she said—

"It is a long time since I have felt so ill, Beatrix. Remember this, darling, my papers are in the black cabinet in my bed-room at home—I mean Wardlock. There is not a great deal. My jointure stops, you know; but whatever little there is, is for you, darling."

"You're not to talk of it, granny, darling, you'll be quite well in a minute; the air is doing you good. May I give you a little wine?— Well, a little water?"

"Thanks, dear; I *am* better. Remember what I told you, and particularly your promise to mention what you heard to no one. I mean the—the—strange scene with that young man. I think I will take a glass of wine. I'll tell you all when I'm better—when Monsieur Varbarriere comes back. It is important for a time, especially having heard what I have, that I should wait a little."

Granny sipped a little sherry slowly, and the tint of life, such as visits the cheek of the aged, returned to hers, and she was better.

"I'd rather not see him any more. It's all like a dream. I don't know what to make of it," muttered granny; and she began audibly to repeat passages, tremblingly and with upturned eyes, from her prayer-book.

Perplexed, anxious, excited, Beatrix looked down on the collapsed and haggard face of the old lady, and listened to the moaned petition, "Lord, have mercy upon us!" which trembled from her lips as it might from those of a fainting sinner on a death-bed.

Guy Deverell, as I shall henceforward call him, thinking of nothing but escape into solitude, was soon a good way from the house. He was too much agitated, and his thoughts too confused at first, to estimate all the possible consequences of the sudden disclosure he had just made.

What would Varbarriere, who could be stern and violent, say or do, when he learned it? Here was the one injunction on which he had been ever harping violated. He felt how much he owed to the unceasing care of that able and disinterested friend through all his life, and how had he repaid it all!

"Anything but deception—anything but that. I could not endure the agony of my position longer—yes, agony."

He was now wandering by the bank of the solitary river, and looked back at the picturesque gables of Marlowe Manor through the trees; and he felt that he was leaving all that could possibly interest him in existence in leaving Marlowe. Always was rising in his mind the one thought, "What does she think of my deception and my agitation—what can she think of *me*?"

It is not easy, even in silence and alone, when the feelings are at all ruffled, to follow out a train of thought. Guy thought of his approaching farewell to his uncle: he sometimes heard his great voice thundering in despair and fury over his ruined schemes—schemes, be they what they might, at least unselfish. Then he thought of the effect of the discovery on Sir Jekyl, who, no doubt, had special reasons for alarm connected with this name—a secret so jealously guarded by Varbarriere. Then he thought of his future. His commission in the French army awaited him. A life of drudgery or listlessness? No such thing! a career of adventure and glory—ending in a baton or death! Death is so romantic in the field! There are always some beautiful eyes to drop in secret those tears which are worth dying for. It is not a crowded trench, where fifty corpses pig together in the last noisome sleep—but an apotheosis!

He was sure he had done well in yielding to the impulse that put an end to the tedious treachery he had been doomed to practise; and if well, then *wisely*—so, no more retrospection.

All this rose and appeared in fragments like a wreck in the eddies of his mind.

One thing was clear—he must leave Marlowe forthwith. He could not meet his host again. He stood up. It is well to have hit upon anything to be done—anything quite certain.

With rapid steps he now returned to Marlowe, wondering how far he had walked, as it seemed to him, in so mere a moment of time.

The house was deserted; so fine a day had tempted all its inmates but old Lady Alice abroad. He sent to the village of Marlowe for a chaise, while Jacques, who was to await where he was the return of his master, Monsieur Varbarriere, got his luggage into readiness, and he himself wrote, having tried and torn up half a dozen, a note to Sir Jekyl, thanking him for his hospitality, and regretting that an unexpected occurrence made his departure on so short notice unavoidable. He did not sign it. He would not write his assumed name. Sir Jekyl could have no difficulty in knowing from which of his guests it came, perhaps would not even miss the signature.

The chaise stood at the door-steps, his luggage stowed away, his dark short travelling cloak about his shoulders, and his note to Sir Jekyl in his fingers.

He entered the great hall, meaning to place it on the marble table where Sir Jekyl's notes and newspapers usually awaited him, and there he encountered Beatrix.

There was no one else. She was crossing to the outer door, and they almost met before they came to a stop.

"Oh! Mr. Strangways."

"Pray call me by my real name, Deverell. Strangways was my mother's; and in obedience to those who are wiser than I, during my journey I adopted it, although the reasons were not told me."

There was a little pause here.

"I am very glad I was so fortunate as to meet you, Miss Marlowe, before I left. I'm just going, and it would be such a privilege to know that you had not judged me very hardly."

"I'm sure papa will be very sorry you are going—a break-up is always a sad event—we miss our guests so much," she said, smiling, but a little pale.

"If you knew my story, Miss Marlowe, you would acquit me," he said, bursting forth all at once. "Misfortune overtook me in my early childhood, before I can remember. I have no right to trouble you with the recital; and in my folly I superadded this—the worst—that madly I gave my love to one who could not return it—who, perhaps, ought not to have returned it. Pardon me, Miss Marlowe, for talking of these things; but as I am going away, and wished you to understand me, I thought, perhaps, you would hear me. Seeing how hopeless was my love, I never told it, but resolved to see her no more, and so to the end of my days will keep my vow; but this is added, that for her sake my life becomes a sacrifice—a real one—to guard her from sorrows and dangers, which I believe *did* threaten her, and to save her from which I devote myself, as perhaps she will one day understand. I thought I would just tell you so much before I went, and—and—that *you* are that lady. Farewell, dear Miss Marlowe, most beautiful—beloved."

He pressed her hand, he kissed it passionately, and was gone.

It was not until she had heard the vehicle drive rapidly away that she quite recovered herself. She went into the front hall, and, through the window, standing far back, watched the receding chaise. When it was out of sight, humming a gay air, she ran up-stairs, and into her bed-room, when, locking the door, she wept the bitterest tears, perhaps, she had ever shed, since the days of her childhood.

CHAPTER VI.

At the Bell and Horns.

With the reader's permission, I must tell here how Monsieur Varbarriere proceeded on his route to Slowton.

As he mounted his vehicle from the steps of Wardlock, the flunky, who was tantalised by the very unsatisfactory result of his listening at the parlour-door, considered him curiously.

"Go on towards the village," said M. Varbarriere to the driver, in his deep foreign accents.

And so soon as they were quite out of sight of the Wardlock flunky, he opened the front window of his nondescript vehicle, and called—

"Drive to Slowton."

Which, accordingly, was done. M. Varbarriere, in profound good-humour, a flood of light and certainty having come upon him, sat back luxuriously in a halo of sardonic glory, and was smiling to himself, as men sometimes will over the chess-board when the rest of their game is secure.

At the Bell and Horns he was received with a reverential welcome.

"A gentleman been inquiring for Monsieur Varbarriere?" asked the foreign gentleman in black, descending.

"A gentleman, sir, as has took number seven, and expects a gentleman to call, but did not say who, which his name is Mr. Rumsey?"

"Very good," said Monsieur Varbarriere.

Suddenly he recollected that General Lennox's letter might have reached the post-office, and, plucking a card from his case, wrote an order on it for his letters, which he handed to Boots, who trudged away to the post-office close by.

Varbarriere was half sorry now that he had opened his correspondence with old General Lennox so soon. He had no hope that Donica Gwynn's reserves would have melted and given way so rapidly in the interview which had taken place. He was a man who cared nothing about penal justice, who had embraced the world's ethics early, and looked indulgently on escapades of human nature, and had no natural turn for cruelty, although he could be cruel enough when an object was to be accomplished.

"I don't think I'd have done it, though he deserves it richly, and has little right to look for quarter at my hands."

And whichever of the gentlemen interested he may have alluded to, he cursed him under his breath ardently.

In number seven there awaited him a tall and thin man of business, of a sad countenance and bilious, with a pale drab-coloured and barred muslin cravat, tied with as much precision as a curate's; a little bald at the very top of his head; a little stooped at his shoulders. He did not smile as Monsieur Varbarriere entered the room. He bowed in a meek and suffering way, and looked as if he had spent the morning in reading Doctor Blewish's pamphlet "On the Ubiquity of Disguised Cholera Morbus," or our good Bishop's well-known tract on "Self-Mortification." There was a smell of cigars in the room, which should not have been had he known that Monsieur Varbarriere was to be here so early. His chest was weak, and the doctors ordered that sort of fumigation.

Monsieur Varbarriere set his mind at ease by preparing himself to smoke one of the notable large cigars, of which he carried always a dozen rounds or so in his case.

"You have brought the cases and opinions with you?" inquired Varbarriere.

The melancholy solicitor replied by opening a tin box, from which he drew several sheafs of neatly labelled papers tied up in red tape; the most methodical and quiet of attorneys, and one of the most efficient to be found.

"Smoke away; you like it, so do I; we can talk too, and look at these," said Varbarriere, lighting his cigar.

Mr. Rumsey bowed, and meekly lighted his also.

Then began the conference on business.

"Where are Gamford's letters?—these?—ho!"

And as Monsieur Varbarriere read them, puffing away as fast as a furnace, and threw each down as he would play a card, in turn, he would cry "Bah!"—"Booh!"—or, "Did you ever read such Galamathias?"—and, at last—

"Who was right about that *benet*—you or I? I told you what he was."

"You will perceive just now, I think, sir, that there are some things of value there notwithstanding. You can't see their importance until you shall have looked into the enlarged statement we have been enabled by the result of some fresh discoveries to submit to counsel."

"Give me that case. Fresh discoveries, have you? I venture to say, when you've heard my notes, you'll open your eyes. No, I mean the cigar-case; well, you may give me that too."

So he took the paper, with its bluish briefing post pages, and broad margin, and the opinions of Mr. Serjeant Edgeways and Mr. Whaulbane, Q.C., copied in the same large, round hand at the conclusion.

"Well, these opinions are stronger than I expected. There is a bit here in Whaulbane's I don't like so well—what you call fishy, you know. But you shall hear just now what I can add to our proofs, and you will see what becomes of good Mr. Whaulbane's doubts and queries. You said always you did not think they had destroyed the deed?"

"If well advised, they did not. I go that length. Because the deed, although it told against them while a claimant in the Deverell line appeared, would yet be an essential part of their case in the event of their title being attacked from the Bracton quarter; and therefore the fact is, they could not destroy it."

"They are both quite clear upon the question of secondary evidence of the contents of a lost deed, I see," said Varbarriere, musingly, "and think our proof satisfactory. Those advocates, however—*why* do they?—always say their say with so many reserves and misgivings, that you begin to think they know very little more of the likelihoods of the matter, with all their pedantry, than you do yourself."

"The glorious uncertainty of the law!" ejaculated Mr. Rumsey, employing a phrase which I have heard before, and with the nearest approach to a macerated smile which his face had yet worn.

"Ay," said Varbarriere, in his metallic tones of banter, "the glorious uncertainty of the law. That must be true, for you're always saying it; and it must be pleasant too, if one could only see it; for, my faith! you look almost cheerful while you say it."

"It makes counsel cautious, though it does not cool clients when they're once fairly blooded," said Mr. Rumsey. "A client is a wonderful thing sometimes. There would not be half the money made of our profession if men kept their senses when they go into law; but they seldom do. Lots of cool gamblers at every other game, but no one ever keeps his head at law."

"That's encouraging; thank you. Suppose I take your advice, and draw stakes?" said Varbarriere.

"You have no notion," said Mr. Rumsey, resignedly.

"Well, I believe you're right, monsieur; and I believe *I* am right too; and if you have any faith in your favourite oracles, so must you; but, have you done your cigar? Well, take your pen for a moment and listen to me, and note what I say. When Deverell came down with his title-deeds to Marlowe, they gave him the Window dressing-room for his bed-room, and the green chamber, with the bed taken down, for his dressing-room; and there he placed his papers, with the key turned in the door. In the morning his attorney came. It was a meeting about a settlement of the mortgage; and when the papers were overhauled it was found that that deed had been abstracted. Very good. Now listen to what I have to relate concerning the peculiar construction of that room."

So Monsieur Varbarriere proceeded to relate minutely all he had ascertained that day, much to the quiet edification of Mr. Rumsey, whose eyes brightened, and whose frontal wrinkles deepened as he listened.

"I told you I suspected some legerdemain about that room long ago; the idea came to me oddly. When on a visit to the Marquis de Mirault he told me that in making alterations in the chateau they had discovered a false door into one of the bed-rooms. The tradition of this contrivance, which was singularly artful, was lost. It is possible that the secret of it perished with its first possessor. By means of this door the apartment in question was placed in almost immediate conjunction with another, which, except through this admirably concealed door, could not be reached from it without a long circuit. The proximity of the rooms, in fact, had been, by reason of the craft with which they were apparently separated, entirely overlooked."

The attorney observed, sadly—

"The French are an ingenious people."

"The curiosity of my friend was excited," continued Varbarriere, "and with some little search among family records he found that this room, which was constructed in the way of an addition to the chateau, had been built about the beginning of the eighteenth century, during the marquisate of one of the line, who was celebrated as *un homme à bonnes fortunes*, you understand, and its object was now quite palpable."

"A man, no doubt, of ability—a long-headed gentleman," mused the melancholy attorney.

"Well, at Marlowe I saw a collection of elevations of the green chamber, as it is called, built only two or three years later—and, mind this, by the same architect, an Italian, called Paulo Abruzzi, a remarkable name, which I perfectly remembered as having been mentioned by my friend the Marquis as the architect of his ancestral relic of Cupid's legerdemain. But here is the most remarkable circumstance, and to which my friend Sir Jekyl quite innocently gave its proper point. The room under this chamber, and, of course, in the same building, was decorated with portraits painted in the panel, and one of them was this identical Marquis de Mirault, with the date 1711, and the Baronet was good enough to tell me that he had been a very intimate friend, and had visited his grandfather, at Marlowe."

CHAPTER VII.

M. Varbarriere's Plans.

Varbarriere solemnly lighted a cigar, and squinted at its glowing point with his great dark eyes, in which the mild attorney saw the lurid reflection. When it was well lighted he went on—

"You may suppose how this confirmed my theory. I set about my inquiries quietly, and was convinced that Sir Jekyl knew all about it, by his disquietude whenever I evinced an interest in that portion of the building. But I managed matters very slyly, and collected proof very nearly demonstrative; and at this moment he has not a notion who I am."

"No. It will be a surprise when he does learn," answered the attorney, sadly.

"A fine natural hair-dye is the air of the East Indies: first it turns light to black, and then black to grey. Then, my faith!—a bronzed face with plenty of furrows, a double chin, and a great beard to cover it, and eleven stone weight expanded to seventeen stone—*Corpo di Bacco!*—and six pounds!"

And Monsieur Varbarriere laughed like the clang and roar of a chime of cathedral bells.

"It will be a smart blow," said the attorney, almost dreamily.

"Smash him," said Varbarriere. "The Deverell estate is something over five thousand a-year; and the mesne rates, with four per cent. interest, amount to 213,000*l.*"

"He'll defend it," said the knight of the sorrowful countenance, who was now gathering in his papers.

"I hope he will," growled Varbarriere, with a chuckle. "He has not a leg to stand on—all the better for *you*, at all events; and then I'll bring down that other hammer on his head."

"The criminal proceedings?" murmured the sad attorney.

"Ay. I can prove that case myself—he fired before his time, and killed him, I'm certain simply to get the estate. I was the only person present—poor Guy! Jekyl had me in his pocket then. The rascal wanted to thrust me down and destroy me afterwards. He employed that Jew house, Röbenzahl and Isaacs—the villain! Luck turned, and I am a rich fellow now, and his turn is coming. Vive la justice éternelle! Vive la bagatelle! Bravo! Bah!"

Monsieur Varbarriere had another pleasant roar of laughter here, and threw his hat at the solemn attorney's head.

"You'll lunch with me," said Varbarriere.

"Thanks," murmured the attorney.

"And now the war—the campaign—what next?"

"You'll make an exact note," the attorney musingly replied, "of what that woman Wynn or Gwynn can prove; also what the Lord Bishop of what's-his-name can prove; and it strikes me we shall have to serve some notice to intimidate Sir Jekyl about that red-leather box, to prevent his making away with the deed, and show him we know it is there; or perhaps apply for an order to make him lodge the deed in court; but Tom Weavel—he's always in town—will advise us. You don't think that woman will leave us in the lurch?"

"No," said Varbarriere, as if he was thinking of something else. "That Donica Gwynn, you mean. She had that green chamber to herself, you see, for a matter of three years."

"Yes."

"And she's one of those old domestic Dianas who are sensitive about scandal—you understand—and she knows what ill-natured people would say; so I quieted her all I could, and I don't think she'll venture to recede. No; she certainly won't."

"How soon can you let me have the notes, sir?"

"To-morrow, when I return. I've an appointment to keep by rail to-night, and I'll make a full memorandum from my notes as I go along."

"Thanks—and what are your instructions?"

"Send back the cases with copies of the new evidence."

"And assuming a favourable opinion, sir, are my instructions to proceed?"

"Certainly, my son, forthwith—the grass it must not grow under our feet."

"Of course subject to counsel's opinion?" said the attorney, sadly.

"To be sure."

"And which first—the action or the indictment? or both together?" asked Mr. Rumsey.

"*That* for counsel too. Only my general direction is, let the onset be as sudden, violent, and determined as possible. You see?"

The attorney nodded gently, tying up his last bundle of papers as softly as a lady might knot her ribbon round the neck of her lap-dog.

"You see?"

"Yes, sir; your object is destruction. Delenda est Carthago—that's the word," murmured Mr. Rumsey, plaintively.

"Yes—ha, ha!—what you call double him up!" clanged out Varbarriere, with an exulting oath and a chuckle.

The attorney had locked up his despatch-box now, and putting the little bunch of keys deep into his trowsers pocket, he said, "Yes, that's the word; but I suppose you have considered—"

"*What?* I'm tired considering."

"I was going to say whether some more certain result might not be obtainable by negotiation; that is, if you thought it a case for negotiation."

"*What* negotiation? What do you mean?"

"Well, you see there are materials—there's something to yield at both sides," said the attorney, very slowly, in a diplomatic reverie.

"But why should you think of a compromise?—the worst thing I fancy could happen to *you*."

There was a general truth in this. It is not the ferryman's interest to build a bridge, nor was it Mr. Rumsey's that his client should walk high and dry over those troubled waters through which it was his privilege and profit to pilot him. But he had not quite so much faith in this case as Monsieur Varbarriere had, and he knew that his wealthy and resolute client could grow savage enough in defeat, and had once or twice had stormy interviews with him after failures.

"If the young gentleman and young lady liked one another, for instance, the conflicting claims might be reconciled, and a marriage would in that case arrange the difference."

"There's nothing very deep in that," snarled Varbarriere, "but there is everything impracticable. Do you think Guy Deverell, whose father that *lache* murdered before my eyes, could ever endure to call *him* father? Bah! If I thought so I would drive him from my presence and never behold him more. No, no, no! There is more than an estate in all this—there is justice, there is *punishment*."

Monsieur Varbarriere, with his hands in his pockets, took a turn up and down the room, and his solemn steps shook the floor, and his countenance was agitated by violence and hatred.

The pale, thin attorney eyed him with a gentle and careworn observation. His respected client was heaving with a great toppling swagger as he to-ed and fro-ed in his thunderstorm, looking as black as the Spirit of Evil.

This old-maidish attorney was meek and wise, but by no means timid. He was accustomed to hear strong language, and sometimes even oaths, without any strange emotion. He looked on this sort of volcanic demonstration scientifically, as a policeman does on drunkenness—knew its stages, and when it was best left to itself.

Mr. Rumsey, therefore, poked the fire a little, and then looked out of the window.

"You don't go to town to-night?"

"Not if you require me here, sir."

"Yes, I shall have those memoranda to give you—and tell me now, I think you know your business. Do you think, as we now stand, success is *certain*?"

"Well, sir, it certainly is very strong—very; but I need not tell you a case will sometimes take a queer turn, and I never like to tell a client that anything is absolutely certain—a case is sometimes carried out of its legitimate course, you see; the judges may go wrong, or the jury bolt, or a witness may break down, or else a bit of evidence may start up—it's a responsibility we never take on ourselves to say that of any case; and you know there has been a good deal of time—and that sometimes raises a feeling with a jury."

"Ay, a quarter of a century, but it can't be helped. For ten years of that time I could not show, I owed money to everybody. Then, when *I* was for striking on the criminal charge for *murder*, or *manslaughter*, or whatever you agreed it was to be, you all said I must begin with the civil action, and first oust him from Guy Deverell's estate. Well, *there* you told me I could not move till he was twenty-five, and now you talk of the good deal of time—*ma foi!*—as if it was I who delayed, and not *you*, messieurs. But enough, past is past. We have the present, and I'll use it."

"We are to go on, then?"

"Yes, we've had to wait too long. Stop for nothing, drive right on, you see, at the fastest pace counsel can manage. If I saw the Deverell estate where it should be, and a judgment for the mesne rates, and Sir Jekyl Marlowe in the dock for his crime, I don't say I should sing *nunc dimittis*; but, *parbleu*, sir, it would be very agreeable—ha! ha! ha!"

CHAPTER VIII.

Tempest.

"Does Mr. Guy Deverell know anything of the measures you contemplate in his behalf?" inquired the attorney.

"Nothing. Do you think me a fool? Young men *are* such asses!"

"You know, however, of course, that he will act. The proceedings, you know, must be in his name."

"Leave that to me."

Varbarriere rang the bell and ordered luncheon. There were grouse and trout—he was in luck—and some cream cheese, for which rural delicacy he had a fancy. They brew very great ale at Slowton, like the Welsh, and it was a novelty to the gentleman of foreign habits, who eat as fastidiously as a Frenchman, and as largely as a German. On the whole it was satisfactory, and the high-shouldered, Jewish-looking sybarite shook hands in a very friendly way with his attorney in the afternoon, on the platform at Slowton, and glided off toward Chester, into which ancient town he thundered, screaming like a monster rushing on its prey; and a victim awaited him in the old commercial hotel; a tall, white-headed military-looking man, with a white moustache twirled up fiercely at the corners; whose short pinkish face and grey eyes, as evening deepened, were pretty constantly presented at the window of the coffee-room next the street door of the inn. From that post he saw all the shops and gas-lamps, up and down the street, gradually lighted. The gaselier in the centre of the coffee-room, with its six muffed glass globes, flared up over the rumpled and coffee-stained morning newspapers and the almanac, and the battered and dissipated-looking railway guide, with corners curled and back coming to pieces, which he consulted every ten minutes through his glasses.

How many consultations he had had with the waiter upon the arrival of trains due at various hours, and how often the injunction had been repeated to see that no mistake occurred about the private room he had ordered; and how reiterated the order that any gentleman inquiring for General Lennox should be shown at once into his presence, the patient waiter with the bilious complexion could tell.

As the time drew near, the General having again conferred with the waiter, conversed with the porter, and even talked a little with Boots—withdrew to his small square sitting-room and pair of candles up-stairs, and awaited the arrival of Monsieur Varbarriere, with his back to the fire, in a state of extreme fidget.

That gentleman's voice he soon heard upon the passage, and the creaking of his heavy tread; and he felt as he used, when a young soldier, on going into action.

The General stepped forward. The waiter announced a gentleman who wished to see him; and Varbarriere's dark visage and mufflers, and sable mantle loomed behind; his felt hat in his hand, and his wavy cone of grizzled hair was bowing solemnly.

"Glad you're come—how d'ye do?" and Varbarriere's fat brown hand was seized by the General's pink and knotted fingers in a very cold and damp grasp. "Come in and sit down, sir. What will you take?—tea, or dinner, or what?"

"Very much obliged. I have ordered something, by-and-by, to my room—thank you very much. I thought, however, that you might possibly wish to see me immediately, and so I am here, at all events, as you soldiers say, to report myself," said Varbarriere, with his unctuous politeness.

"Yes, it *is* better, I'd rather have it now," answered the General in a less polite and more literal way. "A chair, sir;" and he placed one before the fire, which he poked into a blaze. "I—I hope you are not fatigued,"—here the door shut, and the waiter was gone; "and I want to hear, sir, if you please, the—the meaning of the letter you favoured me with."

The General by this time had it in his hand open, and tendered it, I suppose for identification, to M. Varbarriere, who, however, politely waved it back.

"I quite felt the responsibility I took upon myself when I wrote as I did. That responsibility of course I accept; and I have come all this way, sir, for no other purpose than to justify my expressions, and to invite you to bring them to the test."

"Of *course*, sir. Thank you," said the General.

Varbarriere had felt a momentary qualm about this particular branch of the business which he had cut out for himself. When he wrote to General Lennox he was morally *certain* of the existence of a secret passage into that green room, and also of the relations which he had for some time suspected between Sir Jekyl and his fair guest. On the whole it was not a bad *coup* to provide, by means of the old General's jealousy, such literal proof as he still required of the concealed entrance, through which so much villany had been accomplished—and so his letter—and now its consequences—about which it was too late to think.

General Lennox, standing by the table, with one candle on the chimneypiece and his glasses to his eyes, read aloud, with some little stumbling, these words from the letter of Monsieur Varbarriere:—

"The reason of my so doing will be obvious when I say that I have certain circumstances to lay before you which nearly affect your honour. I decline making any detailed statement by letter; nor will I explain my meaning at Marlowe Manor. But if, without *fracas*, you will give me a private meeting, at any place between this and London, I will make it my business to see you, when I shall satisfy you that I have not made this request without the gravest reasons."

"Those are the passages, sir, on which you are so good as to offer me an explanation; and first, there's the phrase, you know, 'certain circumstances to lay before you which nearly affect your *honour*;' that's a word, you know, sir, that a fellow *feels* in a way—in a way that can't be triffled with."

"Certainly. Put your question, General Lennox, how you please," answered Varbarriere, with a grave bow.

"Well, how—how—exactly—I'll—I will put my question. I'd like to know, sir, in what relation—in—yes—in what relation, as a soldier, sir, or as a gentleman, sir, or as—*what*?"

"I am very much concerned to say, sir, that it is in the very nearest and most sacred interest, sir—as a *husband*."

General Lennox had sat down by this time, and was gazing with a frank stern stare full into the dark countenance of his visitor; and in reply he made two short little nods, clearing his voice, and lowering his eyes to the table.

It was a very trifling way of taking it. But Varbarriere saw his face flush fiercely up to the very roots of his silver hair, and he fancied he could see the vessels throbbing in his temples.

"I—very good, sir—thank you," said the General, looking up fiercely and shaking his ears, but speaking in a calm tone.

"Go on, pray—let me know—I say—in God's name, don't keep me."

"Now, sir, I'll tell it to you briefly—I'll afterwards go into whatever proof you desire. I have reason, I deeply regret it, to believe—in fact to know—that an immoral intimacy exists between Sir Jekyl Marlowe and Lady Jane Lennox."

"It's a lie, sir!" screamed the General—"a damned lie, sir—a damned lie, sir—a *damned* lie, sir."

His gouty claw was advanced trembling as if to clutch the muffler that was folded about Monsieur Varbarriere's throat, but he dropped back in his seat again shaking, and ran his fingers through his white hair several times. There was a silence which even M. Varbarriere did not like.

Varbarriere was not the least offended at his violence. He knew quite well that the General did not understand what he said, or mean, or remember it—that it was only the wild protest of agony. For the first time he felt a compunction about that old foozle, who had hitherto somehow counted for nothing in the game he was playing, and he saw him, years after, as he had shrieked at him that night, with his claw stretched towards his throat, ludicrous, and also terrible.

"My God! sir," cried the old man, with a quaver that sounded like a laugh, "do you tell me so?"

"It's true, sir," said Varbarriere.

"Now, sir, I'll not interrupt you—tell all, pray—hide nothing," said the General.

"I was, sir, accidentally witness to a conversation which is capable of no other interpretation; and I have legal proof of the existence of a secret door, connecting the apartment which has been assigned to you, at Marlowe, with Sir Jekyl's room."

"The damned villain! What a fool," and then very fiercely he suddenly added, "You can prove all this, sir? I hope you can."

"All this, and more, sir. I suspect, sir, there will hardly be an attempt to deny it."

"Oh, sir, it's terrible; but I was such a fool. I had no business—I deserve it all. Who'd have imagined such villains? But, d—— me, sir, I can't believe it."

There was a tone of anguish in the old man's voice which made even his grotesque and feeble talk terrible.

"I say there can't be such devils on earth;" and then he broke into an incoherent story of all his trust and love, and all that Jane owed him, and of her nature which was frank and generous, and how she never hid a thought from him—open as heaven, sir. What business was it of his, d—— him! What did he mean by trying to set a man against his wife? No one but a scoundrel ever did it.

Varbarriere stood erect.

"You may submit how you like, sir, to your fate; but you shan't insult me, sir, without answering it. My note left it optional to you to exact my information or to remain in the darkness, which it seems you prefer. If you wish it, I'll make my bow—it's nothing to me, but two can play at that game. I've fought perhaps oftener than you, and you shan't bully *me*."

"I suppose you're right, sir—don't go, pray—I think I'm half *mad*, sir," said General Lennox, despairingly.

"Sir, I make allowance—I forgive your language, but if you want to talk to me, it must be with proper respect. I'm as good a gentleman as you; my statement is, of course, strictly true, and if you please you can test it."

CHAPTER IX.

Guy Deverell at Slowton.

"Come, sir, I have a right to know it—have you not an object in fooling me?" said General Lennox, relapsing all on a sudden into his ferocious vein.

"In telling you the truth, sir, I *have* an object, perhaps—but seeing that it *is* the truth, and concerns you so nearly, you need not trouble yourself about *my* object," answered Varbarriere, with more self-command than was to have been expected.

"I *will* test it, sir. I will try you," said the General, sternly. "By — — I'll sift it to the bottom."

"So you ought, sir; that's what I mean to help you to," said Varbarriere.

"How, sir?—say *how*, and by Heaven, sir, I'll shoot him like a dog."

"The way to do it I've considered. I shall place you *probably* in possession of such proof as will thoroughly convince you."

"Thank you, sir, go on."

"I shall be at Marlowe to-morrow—you must arrive late—on no account earlier than half-past twelve. I will arrange to have you admitted by the glass door—through the conservatory. Don't bring your vehicle beyond the bridge, and leave your luggage at the Marlowe Arms. The object, sir, is this," said Varbarriere, with deliberate emphasis, observing that the General's grim countenance did not look as apprehensive as he wished, "that your arrival shall be unsuspected. No one must know anything of it except myself and another, until you shall have reached your room. Do you see?"

"Thanks, sir—yes," answered the General, looking as unsatisfactorily as before.

"There are two recesses with shelves—one to the right, the other to the left of the bed's head as you look from the door. The secret entrance I have mentioned lies through that at the right. You must not permit any alarm which may be intended to reach Sir Jekyl. Secure the door, and do you sit up and watch. There's a way of securing the secret door from the inside—which I'll explain—that would *prevent* his entrance—don't allow it. The whole—pardon me, sir—*intrigue* will in that case be disclosed without the possibility of a prevarication. You have followed me, I hope, distinctly."

"I—I'm a little flurried, I believe, sir; I have to apologise. I'll ask you, by-and-by, to repeat it. I think I should like to be alone, sir. She wrote me a letter, sir—I wish I had died when I got it."

When Varbarriere looked at him, he saw that the old East Indian was crying.

"Sir, I grieve with you," said Varbarriere, funereally. "You can command my presence whenever you please to send for me. I shall remain in this house. It will be absolutely necessary, of course, that you should see me again."

"Thank you, sir. I know—I'm sure you mean kindly—but God only knows all it is."

He had shaken his hand very affectionately, without any meaning—without knowing that he had done so.

Varbarriere said—

"Don't give way, sir, too much. If there is this sort of misfortune, it is much better discovered—*much* better. You'll think so just now. You'll view it quite differently in the morning. Call for me the moment you want me—farewell, sir."

So Varbarriere was conducted to his bed-room, and made, beside his toilet, conscientious inquiries about his late dinner, which was in an advanced state of preparation; and when he went down to partake of it, he had wonderfully recovered the interview with General Lennox.

Notwithstanding, however, he drank two glasses of sherry, contrary to gastronomic laws, before beginning. Then, however, he made, even for him, a very good dinner.

He could not help wondering what a prodigious fuss the poor old fogey made about this little affair. He could not enter the least into his state of mind. She was a fine woman, no doubt; but there were others—no stint—and he had been married quite long enough to sober and acquire an appetite for liberty.

What was the matter with the old fellow? But that it was insufferably comical, he could almost find it in his heart to pity him.

Once or twice as he smoked his cigar he could not forbear shaking with laughter, the old Philander's pathetics struck him so sardonically.

I really think the state of that old gentleman, who certainly had attained to years of philosophy, was rather serious. That is, I dare say that a competent medical man with his case under observation at that moment would have pronounced him on the verge either of a fit or of insanity.

When Varbarriere had left the room, General Lennox threw himself on the red damask sofa, which smelled powerfully of yesterday's swell bagman's tobacco, never perceiving that stale fragrance, nor the thinness of the cushion which made the ribs and vertebræ of the couch unpleasantly perceptible beneath. Then, with his knees doubled up, and the "Times" newspaper over his face, he wept, and moaned, and uttered such plaintive and hideous maunderings as would do nobody good to hear of.

A variety of wise impulses visited him. One was to start instantaneously for Marlowe and fight Sir Jekyl that night by candlelight; another, to write to his wife for the last time as his wife—an eternal farewell—which perhaps would have been highly absurd, and affecting at the same time.

About two hours after Varbarriere's departure for dinner, he sent for that gentleman, and they had another, a longer, and a more collected interview—if not a happier one.

The result was, that Varbarriere's advice prevailed, as one might easily foresee, having a patient so utterly incompetent to advise himself.

The attorney, having shaken hands with Monsieur Varbarriere, and watched from the platform the gradual disappearance of the train that carried him from the purlieus of Slowton, with an expression of face plaintive as that with which Dido on the wild sea banks beheld the receding galleys of Æneas, loitered back again dolorously to the hostelry.

He arrived at the door exactly in time to witness the descent of Guy Deverell from his chaise. I think he would have preferred not meeting him, it would have saved him a few boring questions; but it was by no means a case for concealing himself. He therefore met him with a melancholy frankness on the steps.

The young man recognised him.

"Mr. Rumsey?—How do you do? Is my uncle here?"

"He left by the last train. I hope I see you well, sir."

"Gone? and where to?"

"He did not tell me." That was true, but the attorney had seen his valise labelled "Chester" by his direction. "He went by the London train, but he said he would be back to-morrow. Can *I* do anything? Your arrival was not expected."

"Thank you. I think not. It was just a word with my uncle I wished. You say he will be here again in the morning?"

"Yes, so he said. I'm waiting to see him."

"Then I can't fail to meet him if I remain." The attorney perceived, with his weatherwise experience, the traces of recent storm, both in the countenance and the manner of this young man, whose restiveness just now might be troublesome.

"Unless your business is urgent, I think—if you'll excuse me—you had better return to Marlowe," remarked the attorney. "You'll find it more comfortable quarters, a good deal, and your uncle will be very much hurried while here, and means to return to Marlowe to-morrow evening."

"But I shan't. I don't mean to return; in fact, I wish to speak to him here. I've delayed you on the steps, sir, very rudely; the wind is cold."

So he bowed, and they entered together, and the attorney, whose curiosity was now a little piqued, found he could make nothing of him, and rather disliked him; his reserve was hardly fair in so very young a person, and practised by one who had not yet won his spurs against so redoubted a champion as the knight of the rueful countenance.

Next morning, as M. Varbarriere had predicted, General Lennox, although sleep had certainly had little to do with the change, was quite a different man in some respects—in no wise happier, but much more collected; and now he promptly apprehended and retained Monsieur Varbarriere's plan, which it was agreed was to be executed that night.

More than once Varbarriere's compunctions revisited him as he sped onwards that morning from Chester to Slowton. But as men will, he bullied these misgivings and upbraidings into submission. He had been once or twice on the point of disclosing this portion of the complication to his attorney, but an odd sort of shyness prevented. He fancied that possibly the picture and his part in it were not altogether pretty, and somehow he did not care to expose himself to the secret action of the attorney's thoughts.

Even in his own mind it needed the strong motive which had first prompted it. Now it was no longer necessary to explore the mystery of that secret door through which the missing deed, and indeed the Deverell estate, had been carried into old Sir Harry's cupboard. But what was to be done? He had committed himself to the statement. General Lennox had a right to demand—in fact, *he* had promised— a distinct explanation.

Yes, a distinct explanation, and, further, a due corroboration by proof of that explanation. It was all due to Monsieur Varbarriere, who had paid that debt to his credit and conscience, and behold what a picture! Three familiar figures, irrevocably transformed, and placed in what a halo of infernal light.

"The thing could not be helped, and, whether or no, it was only right. Why the devil should I help Jekyl Marlowe to deceive and disgrace that withered old gentleman? I don't think it would have been a pleasant position for me."

And all the respectabilities hovering near cried "hear, hear, hear!" and Varbarriere shook up his head, and looked magisterial over the havoc of the last livid scene of the tragedy he had prepared; and the porter crying "Slowton!" opened the door, and released him.

CHAPTER X.

Uncle and Nephew.

When he reached his room, having breakfasted handsomely in the coffee-room, and learned that early Mr. Rumsey had accomplished a similar meal in his own sitting-room, he repaired thither, and entered forthwith upon their talk.

It was a bright and pleasant morning; the poplar trees in front of the hotel were all glittering in the mellow early sunlight, and the birds twittering as pleasantly as if there was not a sorrow or danger on earth.

"Well, sir, true to my hour," said Monsieur Varbarriere, in his deep brazen tones, as smiling and wondrously he entered the attorney's apartment.

"Good morning, sir—how d'ye do? Have you got those notes prepared you mentioned?"

"That I have, sir, as you shall see, pencil though; but that doesn't matter—no?"

The vowel sounded grandly in the upward slide of Varbarriere's titanic double bass.

The attorney took possession of the pocket-book containing these memoranda, and answered—

"No, I can read it very nicely. Your nephew is here, by-the-bye; he came last night."

"Guy? What's brought him here?"

M. Varbarriere's countenance was overcast. What had gone wrong? Some chamber in his mine had exploded, he feared, prematurely.

Varbarriere opened the door, intending to roar for Guy, but remembering where he was, and the dimensions of the place, he tugged instead at the bell-rope, and made his summons jangle wildly through the lower regions.

"Hollo!" cried Varbarriere from his threshold, anticipating the approaching waiter; "a young gentleman—a Mr. Guy Strangways, arrived last evening?"

"Strangways, please, sir? Strangways? No, sir, I don't think we 'av got no gentleman of that name in the 'ouse, sir."

"But I know you *have*. Go, make out where he is, and let him know that his uncle, Monsieur Varbarriere, has just arrived, and wants to see him—*here*, may I?" with a glance at the attorney.

"Certainly."

"There's some mischief," said Varbarriere, with a lowering glance at the attorney.

"It looks uncommon like it," mused that gentleman, sadly.

"Why doesn't he come?" growled Varbarriere, with a motion of his heel like a stamp. "What do you think he has done? Some cursed sottise."

"Possibly he has proposed marriage to the young lady, and been refused."

"Refused! I hope he has."

At this juncture the waiter returned.

"Well?"

"No, sir, please. No one hin the 'ouse, sir. No such name."

"Are you sure?" asked Varbarriere of the attorney, in an under diapason.

"Perfectly—said he'd wait here for you. I told him you'd be here this morning," answered he, dolorously.

"Go down, sir, and get me a list of the gentlemen in the house. I'll pay for it," said Varbarriere, with an imperious jerk of his hand.

The ponderous gentleman in black was very uneasy, and well he might. So he looked silently out of the window which commands a view of the inn yard, and his eyes wandered over a handsome manure-heap to the chicken-coop and paddling ducks, and he saw three horses' tails in perspective in the chiaro-oscuro of the stable, in the open door of which a groom was rubbing a curb chain. He thought how wisely he had done in letting Guy know so little of his designs. And as he gloomily congratulated himself on his wise reserve, the waiter returned with a slate, and a double column of names scratched on it.

Varbarriere having cast his eye over it, suddenly uttered an oath.

"Number 10—that's the gentleman. Go to number 10, and tell him his uncle wants him here," roared Varbarriere, as if on the point of knocking the harmless waiter down. "Read there!" he thundered, placing the slate, with a clang, before the meek attorney, who read opposite to number 10, "Mr. G. Deverell."

He pursed his mouth and looked up lackadaisically at his glowering client, saying only "Ha!"

A minute after and Guy Deverell in person entered the room. He extended his hand deferentially to M. Varbarriere, who on his part drew himself up black as night, and thrust his hands half way to the elbows in his trowsers pockets, glaring thunderbolts in the face of the contumacious young man.

"You see *that*?" jerking the slate with another clang before Guy. "Did *you* give that name? Look at number *ten*, sir." Varbarriere was now again speaking French.

"Yes, sir, Guy Deverell—my own name. I shall never again consent to go by any other. I had no idea what it might involve—never."

The young man was pale, but quite firm.

"You've broken your word, sir; you have ended your relations with me," said Varbarriere, with a horrible coldness.

"I am sorry, sir—I *have* broken my promise, but when I could not keep it without a worse deception. To the consequences, be they what they may, I submit, and I feel, sir, more deeply than you will ever know all the kindness you have shown me from my earliest childhood until now."

"Infinitely flattered," sneered Varbarriere, with a mock bow. "You have, I presume, disclosed your name to the people at Marlowe as frankly as to those at Slowton?"

"Lady Alice Redcliffe called me by my true name, and insisted it was mine. I could not deny it—I admitted the truth. Mademoiselle Marlowe was present also, and heard what passed. In little more than an hour after this scene I left Marlowe Manor. I did not see Sir Jekyl, and simply addressed a note to him saying that I was called away unexpectedly. I did not repeat to him the disclosure made to Lady Alice. I left that to the discretion of those who had heard it."

"Their *discretion*—very good—and now, Monsieur Guy Deverell, I have *done* with you. I shan't leave you as I took you up, absolutely penniless. I shall so place you as to enable you with diligence to earn your bread without degradation—that is all. You will be so good as to repair forthwith to London and await me at our quarters in St. James's Street. I shall send you, by next post, a cheque to meet expenses in town—no, pray don't thank me; you might have thanked me by your obedience. I shan't do much more to merit thanks. Your train starts from hence, I think, in half an hour."

Varbarriere nodded angrily, and moved his hand towards the door.

"Farewell, sir," said Guy, bowing low, but proudly.

"One word more," said Varbarriere, recollecting suddenly; "you have not arranged a correspondence with any person? answer me on your honour."

"No, sir, on my honour."

"Go, then. Adieu!" and Varbarriere turned from him brusquely, and so they parted.

"Am I to understand, sir," inquired the attorney, "that what has just occurred modifies our instructions to proceed in those cases?"

"Not at all, sir," answered Varbarriere, firmly.

"You see the civil proceedings must all be in the name of the young gentleman—a party who is of age—and you see what I mean."

"I undertake personally the entire responsibility; you are to proceed in the name of Guy Deverell, and what is more, use the utmost despatch, and spare no cost. When shall we open the battle?"

"Why, I dare say next term."

"That is less than a month hence?"

"Yes, sir."

"By my faith, his hands will be pretty full by that time," said Varbarriere, exultingly. "We must have the papers out again. I can give you all this day, up to half-past five o'clock. We must get the new case into shape for counsel. You run up to town this evening. I suspect I shall follow you to-morrow; but I must run over first to Marlowe. I have left my things there, and my servant; and I suppose I must take a civil leave of my enemy—there are courtesies, you know—as your prize-fighters shake hands in the ring."

The sun was pretty far down in the west by the time their sederunt ended. M. Varbarriere got into his short mantle and mufflers, and donned his ugly felt hat, talking all the while in his deep metallic tones, with his sliding cadences and resounding emphases. The polite and melancholy attorney accompanied his nutritious client to the door, and after he had taken his seat in his vehicle, they chatted a little earnestly through the window, agreeing that they had grown very "strong" indeed—anticipating nothing but victory, and in confidential whispers breathing slaughter.

As Varbarriere, with his thick arm stuffed through one of the upholstered leathern loops with which it is the custom to flank the windows of all sorts of carriages, and his large varnished boot on the vacant cushion at the other side, leaned back and stared darkly and dreamily through the plate glass on the amber-tinted landscape, he felt rather oddly approaching such persons and such scenes—a crisis with a remoter and more tremendous crisis behind—the thing long predicted in the whisperings of hope—the real thing long dreamed of, and now greeted strangely with a mixture of exultation and disgust.

There are few men, I fancy, who so thoroughly enjoy their revenge as they expected. It is one of those lusts which has its *goût de revers*—"sweet in the mouth, bitter in the belly;" one of those appetites which will allow its victim no rest *till* it is gratified, and no peace *afterward*. Now, M. Varbarriere was in for it, he was already coming under the solemn shadow of its responsibilities, and was chilled. It involved other people, too, besides its proper object—people who, whatever else some of them might be, were certainly, as respected him and his, innocent. Did he quail, and seriously think of retiring *re infectâ*? No such thing! It is wonderful how steadfast of purpose are the disciples of darkness, and how seldom, having put their hands to the plough, they look back.

All this while Guy Deverell, in exile, was approaching London with brain, like every other, teeming with its own phantasmagoria. He knew not what particular danger threatened Marlowe Manor, which to him was a temple tenanted by Beatrix alone, the living idol whom he worshipped. He was assured that somehow his consent, perhaps cooperation, was needed to render the attack effectual, and here would arise his opportunity, the self-sacrifice which he contemplated with positive pleasure, though, of course, with a certain awe, for futurity was a murky vista enough beyond it.

Varbarriere's low estimate of young men led *him* at once to conclude that this was an amorous escapade, a bit of romance about that pretty wench, Mademoiselle Beatrix. Why not? The fool, fooling according to his folly, should not arrest wisdom in her march. Varbarriere was resolved to take all necessary steps in his nephew's name, without troubling the young man with a word upon the subject. He would have judgment and execution, and he scoffed at the idea that his nephew, Guy, would take measures to have him—his kinsman, guardian, and benefactor—punished for having acted for his advantage without his consent.

CHAPTER XI.

In Lady Mary's Boudoir.

The red sunset had faded into darkness as M. Varbarriere descended from his carriage at the door-steps of Marlowe. The dressing-bell had not yet rung. Everyone was quite well, the solemn butler informed him graciously, as if *he* had kept them in health expressly to oblige M. Varbarriere. That gentleman's dark countenance, however, was not specially illuminated on the occasion. The intelligence he really wanted referred to old Lady Alice, to whom the inexcusable folly and perfidy of Guy had betrayed his name.

Upon this point he had grown indescribably uncomfortable as he drew near to the house. Had the old woman been conjecturing and tattling? Had she called in Sir Jekyl himself to counsel? How was he, Varbarriere, to meet Sir Jekyl? He must learn from Lady Alice's lips how the land lay.

"And Lady Alice," he murmured with a lowering countenance, "pretty well, I hope? Down-stairs to-day, eh?"

The butler had not during his entire visit heard the "foreign chap" talk so much English before.

"Lady Halice was well in 'ealth."

"In the drawing-room?"

"No, sir, in Lady Mary's boudoir."

"And Sir Jekyl?"

"In 'is hown room, sir."

"Show me to the boudoir, please; I have a word for Lady Alice."

A few moments more and he knocked at the door of that apartment, and was invited to enter with a querulous drawl that recalled the association of the wild cat with which in an irreverent moment he had once connected that august old lady.

So Varbarriere entered and bowed and stood darkly in the door-frame, reminding her again of the portrait of a fat and cruel burgomaster. "Oh! it's you? come back again, Monsieur Varbarriere? Oh!—I'm very glad to see you."

"Very grateful—very much flattered; and your ladyship, how are *you*?"

"Pretty well—ailing—always ailing—delicate health and *cruelly* tortured in mind. What else can I expect, sir, but sickness?"

"I hope your mind has not been troubled, Lady Alice, since I had the honour of last seeing you."

"Now, *do* you really hope that? Is it *possible* you *can* hope that my mind, in the state in which you left it has been one minute at ease since I saw you? Beside, sir, I have heard something that for reasons quite inexplicable *you* have chosen to conceal from me."

"May I ask what it is? I shall be happy to explain."

"Yes, the name of that young man—it is *not* Strangways, that was a falsehood; his name, sir, is Guy Deverell!"

And saying this Lady Alice, after her wont, wept passionately.

"That is perfectly true, Lady Alice; but I don't see what value that information can have, apart from the explanatory particulars I promised to tell you; but not for a few days. If, however, you desire it, I shall postpone the disclosure no longer. You will, I am sure, first be so good as to tell me, though, whether anyone but you knows that the foolish young man's name is Deverell?"

"No; no one, except Beatrix, not a creature. She was present, but has been, at my request, perfectly silent," answered Lady Alice, eagerly, and gaped darkly at Varbarriere, expecting his revelation.

M. Varbarriere thought, under the untoward circumstances, that a disclosure so imperfect as had been made to Lady Alice was a good deal more dangerous than one a little fuller. He therefore took that lady's hand very reverentially, and looking with his full solemn eyes in her face, said—

"It is not only true, madam, that his name is Guy Deverell, but equally true that he is the lawful son, as well as the namesake, of that Guy Deverell, your *son*, who perished by the hand of Sir Jekyl Marlowe in a duel. Shot down foully, as that Mr. Strangways avers who was his companion, and who was present when the fatal event took place."

"Gracious Heaven, sir! My son married?"

"Yes, madam, *married* more than a year before his death. All the proofs are extant, and at this moment in England."

"Married! my boy married, and never told his mother! Oh, Guy, Guy, *Guy* is it credible?"

"It is not a question, madam, but an absolute certainty, as I will show you whenever I get the papers to Wardlock."

"And to whom, sir, pray, was my son married?" demanded Lady Alice, after a long pause.

"To my sister, madam."

Lady Alice gaped at him in astonishment.

"Was she a person at all his equal in life?—a person of—of any education, I mean?" inquired Lady Alice, with a gasp, sublimely unconscious of her impertinence.

"As good a lady as you are," replied Varbarriere, with a swarthy flush upon his forehead.

"I should like to *know* she was a *lady*, at all events."

"She was a lady, madam, of pure blood, incapable of a mean thought, incapable, too, of anything low-bred or impertinent."

His sarcasm sped through and through Lady Alice without producing any effect, as a bullet passes through a ghost.

"It is a great surprise, sir, but *that* will be satisfactory. I suppose you can show it?"

Varbarriere smiled sardonically and answered nothing.

"My son married to a Frenchwoman! Dear, dear, *dear!* Married! You can feel for me, monsieur, knowing as I do nothing of the person or family with whom he connected himself."

Lady Alice pressed her lean fingers over her heart, and swept the wall opposite, with dismal eyes, sighing at intervals, and gasping dolorously.

The old woman's egotism and impertinence did not vex him long or much. But the pretence of being absolutely above irritation from the feminine gender, in any extant sage, philosopher, or saint, is a despicable affectation. Man and woman were created with inflexible relations; each with the power in large measure or in infinitesimal doses, according to opportunity, to infuse the cup of the other's life with sweet or bitter—with nectar or with poison. Therefore great men and wise men have winced and will wince under the insults of small and even of old women.

"A year, you say, before my poor boy's death?"

"Yes, about that; a little more."

"Mademoiselle Varbarriere! H'm," mused Lady Alice.

"I did not say Varbarriere was the name," sneered he, with a deep-toned drawl.

"Why, you said, sir, did not you, that the Frenchwoman he married was your sister?"

"I said the lady who accepted him was my sister. I never said her name was Varbarriere, or that she was a Frenchwoman."

"Is not your name Varbarriere, sir?" exclaimed Lady Alice, opening her eyes very wide.

"Certainly, madam. A *nom de guerre*, as we say in France, a name which I assumed with the purchase of an estate, about six years ago, when I became what you call a naturalised French subject."

"And pray, sir, what *is* your name?"

"*Varbarriere*, madam. I did bear an English name, being of English birth and family. May I presume to inquire particularly whether you have divulged the name of my nephew to anyone?"

"No, to no one; neither has Beatrix, I am certain."

"You now know, madam, that the young man is your own grandson, and therefore entitled to at least as much consideration from you as from me; and I again venture to impress upon you this fact, that if prematurely his name be disclosed, it may, and indeed *must* embarrass my endeavours to reinstate him in his rights."

As he said this Varbarriere made a profound and solemn bow; and before Lady Alice could resume her catechism, that dark gentleman had left the room.

As he emerged from the door he glanced down the broad oak stair, at the foot of which he heard voices. They were those of Sir Jekyl and his daughter. The Baronet's eye detected the dark form on the first platform above him.

"Ha! Monsieur Varbarriere—very welcome, monsieur—when did you arrive?" cried his host in his accustomed French.

"Ten minutes ago."

"Quite well, I hope."

"Perfectly; many thanks—and Mademoiselle Beatrix?"

The large and sombre figure was descending the stairs all this time, and an awful shadow, as he did so, seemed to overcast the face and form of the young lady, to whom, with a dark smile, he extended his hand.

"Quite well, Beatrix, too—*all* quite well—even Lady Alice in her usual health," said Sir Jekyl.

"*Better*—I'm glad to hear," said Varbarriere.

"Better! Oh dear, no—that would never do. But her temper is just as lively, and all her ailments flourishing. By-the-bye, your nephew had to leave us suddenly."

"Yes—business," said Varbarriere, interrupting.

Beatrix, he was glad to observe, had gone away to the drawing-room.

"He'll be back, I hope, immediately?" continued the Baronet. "He's a fine young fellow. Egad, he's about as good-looking a young fellow as I know. I should be devilish proud of him if I were you. When does he come back to us?"

"Immediately, I hope; business, you know; but nothing very long. We are both, I fear, a very tedious pair of guests; but you have been so pressing, so hospitable——"

"Say rather, so selfish, monsieur," answered Sir Jekyl, laughing. "Our whist and cigars have languished ever since you left."

M. Varbarricrc laughed a double-bass accompaniment to the Baronet's chuckle, and the dressing-bell ringing at that moment, Sir Jekyl and he parted agreeably.

CHAPTER XII.

The Guests Together.

Varbarriere marched slowly up, and entered his dressing-room with a "glooming" countenance and a heavy heart. Everything looked as if he had left it but half an hour ago. He poked the fire and sat down.

He felt like a surgeon with an operation before him. There was a loathing of it, but he did not flinch.

Reader, you think you understand other men. Do you understand yourself? Did you ever quite succeed in defining your own motives, and arriving at the moral base of any action you ever did? Here was Varbarriere sailing with wind and tide full in his favour, right into the haven where he would be—yet to look in his face you would have said "*there* is a sorrowful man," and had you been able to see within, you would have said, "*there* is a man divided against himself." Yes, as every man *is*. Several spirits, quite distinct, not blending, but pleading and battling very earnestly on opposite sides, all in possession of the "house"—but one dominant, always with a disputed sway, but always carrying his point—always the prosperous bully.

Yes, every man is a twist of many strands. Varbarriere was compacted of several Varbarrieres—one of whom was the stronger and the most infernal. His feebler associates commented upon him—despised him—feared him—sought to restrain him but knew they could not. He tyrannised, and was to the outer world the one and indivisible Varbarriere.

Monsieur Varbarriere the tyrant was about to bring about a *fracas* that night, against which the feebler and better Varbarrieres protested. Varbarriere the tyrant held the knife over the throat of a faithless woman—the better Varbarrieres murmured words of pity and of faint remonstrance. Varbarriere the tyrant scrupled not to play the part of spy and traitor for his ends; the nobler Varbarrieres upbraided him sadly, and even despised him. But what were these feeble angelic Varbarrieres? The ruler is the state, *l'état c'est moi!* and Varbarriere the tyrant carried all before him.

As the dark and somewhat corpulent gentleman before the glass adjusted his necktie and viewed his shirt-studs, he saw in his countenance, along with the terrible resolution of that tyrant, the sorrows and fears of the less potent spirits; and he felt, though he would not accept, their upbraidings and their truth; so with a stern and heavy heart he descended to the drawing-room.

He found the party pretty nearly assembled, and the usual buzz and animation prevailing, and he smiled and swayed from group to group, and from one chair to another.

Doocey was glad, monstrous glad to see him.

"I had no idea how hard it was to find a good player, until you left us—our whist has been totally ruined. The first night we tried Linnett; he thinks he plays, you know; well, I do assure you, you never *witnessed* such a thing—such a *caricature*, by Jupiter—forgetting your lead—revoking—*every*thing, by Jove. You may guess what a chance we had—*my* partner, I give you my honour, against old Sir Paul Blunket, as dogged a player as there is in England, egad, and Sir Jekyl there. We tried Drayton next night—the most conceited fellow on earth, and *no head*—Sir Paul had him. I never saw an old fellow so savage. Egad, they were calling one another names across the table—you'd have *died* laughing; but we'll have some play now you've come back, and I'm very glad of it."

Varbarriere, while he listened to all this, smiling his fat dark smile, and shrugging and bowing slightly as the tale required these evidences, was quietly making his observations on two or three of the persons who most interested him. Beatrix, he thought, was looking ill—certainly much paler, and though very pretty, rather sad—that is, she was ever and anon falling into little abstractions, and when spoken to, waking up with a sudden little smile.

Lady Jane Lennox—she did not seem to observe him—was seated like a sultana on a low cushioned seat, with her rich silks circling grandly round her. He looked at her a little stealthily and curiously, as men eye a prisoner who is about to suffer execution. His countenance during that brief glance was unobserved, but you might have read there something sinister and cruel.

"I forget—*had* the Bishop come when you left us?" said Sir Jekyl, laying his hand lightly from behind on the arm of Varbarriere. The dark-featured man winced—Sir Jekyl's voice sounded unpleasantly in his reverie.

"Ah! Oh! The Bishop? Yes—the Bishop was here when I left; he had been here a day or two," answered Varbarriere, with a kind of effort.

"Then I need not introduce you—you're friends already," said Sir Jekyl.

At which moment the assembled party learned that dinner awaited them, and the murmured arrangements for the procession commenced, and the drawing-room was left to the click of the Louis Quatorze clock and the sadness of solitude.

"We had such a dispute, Monsieur Varbarriere, while you were away," said Miss Blunket.

"About me, I hope," answered the gentleman addressed, in tolerable English, and with a gallant jocularity.

"Well, no—not about you," said old Miss Blunket, timidly. "But I so wished for you to take part in the argument."

"And why wish for me?" answered the sardonic old fellow, amused, maybe the least bit in the world flattered.

"Well, I think you have the power, Monsieur Varbarriere, of putting a great deal in very few words—I mean, of making an argument so clear and short."

Varbarriere laughed indulgently, and began to think Miss Blunket a rather intelligent person.

"And what was the subject, pray?"

"Whether life was happier in town or country."

"Oh! the old debate—country mouse against town mouse," replied Varbarriere.

"Ah, just so—so true—I don't think *any*one said that, and—and—I do wish to know which side you would have taken."

"The condition being that it should be all country or all town, of course, and that we were to retain our incomes?"

"Yes, certainly," said Miss Blunket, awaiting his verdict with a little bit of bread suspended between her forefinger and thumb.

"Well, then, I should pronounce at once for the country," said Varbarriere.

"I'm so glad—that's just what I said. I'm sure, said I, I should have Monsieur Varbarriere on my side if he were here. I'm so glad I was right. Did not you hear me say that?" said she, addressing Lady Jane Lennox, whose steady look, obliquely from across the table a little higher up, disconcerted her.

Lady Jane was not thinking of the debate, and asked in her quiet haughty way—

"What is it?"

"Did I not say, yesterday, that Monsieur Varbarriere would vote for the country, in our town or country argument, if he were here?"

"Oh! did you? Yes, I believe you did. I was not listening."

"And which side, pray, Lady Jane, would you have taken in that ancient debate?" inquired Varbarriere, who somehow felt constrained to address her.

"Neither side," answered she.

"What! neither town nor country—and how then?" inquired Varbarriere, with a shrug and a smile.

"I think there is as much hypocrisy and slander in one as the other, and I should have a new way—people living like the Chinese, in boats, and never going on shore."

Varbarriere laughed—twiddled a bit of bread between his finger and thumb, and leaned back, and looked down, still smiling, by the edge of his plate; and was there not a little flush under the dark brown tint of his face?

"That would be simply prison," ejaculated Miss Blunket.

"Yes, prison; and is not anything better than liberty with its liabilities? Why did Lady Hester Stanhope go into exile in the East, and why do sane men and women go into monasteries?"

Varbarriere looked at her with an odd kind of interest, and sighed without knowing it; and he helped himself curiously to sweetbread, a minute later, and for a time his share in the conversation flagged.

Lady Jane, he thought, was looking decidedly better than when he left—very well, in fact—very well indeed—not at all like a person with anything pressing heavily on her mind.

He glanced at her again. She was talking to old Sir Paul Blunket in a bold careless way, which showed no sign of hidden care or fear.

"Have you been to town since?" inquired Sir Jekyl, who happened to catch Varbarriere's eye at that moment, and availed himself of a momentary lull in what we term the conversation, to put his question.

"No; you think I have been pleasuring, but it was good honest business, I assure you."

"Lady Alice here fancied you might have seen the General, and learned something about his plans," continued Sir Jekyl.

"What General?—Lennox—eh?" inquired Varbarriere.

"Yes. What's your question, Lady Alice?" said the Baronet, turning to that lady, and happily not observing an odd expression in Varbarriere's countenance.

"No question; he has not been to London," answered the old lady, drawing her shawl which she chose to dine in about her, chillily.

"Is it anything *I* can answer?" threw in Lady Jane, who, superbly tranquil as she looked, would have liked to pull and box Lady Alice's ears at that moment.

"Oh no, I fancy not; it's only the old question, when are we to see the General; is he coming back at all?"

"I wish anyone could help me to an answer," laughed Lady Jane, with a slight uneasiness, which might have been referred to the pique which would not have been unnatural in a handsome wife neglected.

"I begin to fear I shall leave Marlowe without having seen him," said Lady Alice, peevishly.

"Yes, and it is not complimentary, you know; he disappeared just the day before you came, and he won't come back till you leave; men are such mysterious fellows, don't you think?" said Sir Jekyl.

"It doesn't look as if he liked her company. Did he ever meet you, Lady Alice?" inquired Sir Paul Blunket in his bluff way, without at all intending to be uncivil.

"*That*, you think, would account for it; much obliged to you, Sir Paul," said Lady Alice, sharply.

Sir Paul did not see it, or what she was driving at, and looked at her therefore with a grave curiosity, for he did not perceive that she was offended.

"Sir Paul has a way of hitting people very hard, has not he, Lady Alice? and then leaving them to recover of themselves," said Sir Jekyl.

"There's not a great deal of civility wasted among you," observed Lady Alice.

"I only meant," said Sir Paul, who felt that he should place himself right, "that I could not see why General Lennox should avoid Lady Alice, unless he was acquainted with her. There's nothing in that."

"By-the-bye, Lady Alice," said Sir Jekyl, who apprehended a possible scene from that lady's temper, and like a good shepherd wished to see his flock pasture peaceably together—"I find I can let you have any quantity you like of that plant you admired yesterday. I forget its name, and the Bishop says he has got one at the Palace with a scarlet blossom; so, perhaps, if you make interest with him—what do you say, my lord?"

So having engaged the good Bishop in floral conversation with that fiery spirit, the Baronet asked Sir Paul whether he believed all that was said about the great American cow; and what he thought of the monster parsnip: and thus he set him and Lady Alice ambling on different tracts, so that there was no risk of their breaking lances again.

CHAPTER XIII.

A Visitor in the Library.

The company were now pecking at those fruits over which Sir Jekyl was wont to chuckle grimly, making pleasant satire on his gardener, vowing he kept an Aladdin's garden, and that his greengages were emeralds, and his gooseberries rubies.

In the midst of the talk, the grave and somewhat corpulent butler stood behind his master's chair, and murmured something mildly in his ear.

"What's his name?" inquired Sir Jekyl.

"Pullet, please, sir."

"Pullet! I never heard of him. If he had come a little earlier with a knife and fork in his back, we'd have given a good account of him."

His jokes were chuckled to Lady Alice, who received them drowsily.

"Where have you put him?"

"In the library, please, sir."

"What kind of looking person?"

"A middlish sort of a person, rayther respectable, I should say, sir; but dusty from his journey."

"Well, give him some wine, and let him have dinner, if he has not had it before, and bring in his card just now."

All this occurred without exciting attention or withdrawing Sir Jekyl from any sustained conversation, for he and Lady Alice had been left high and dry on the bank together by the flow and ebb of talk, which at this moment kept the room in a rattle; and Sir Jekyl only now and then troubled her with a word.

"Pullet!" thought Sir Jekyl, he knew not why, uneasily. "Who the devil's Pullet, and what the plague can Pullet want? It can't be Paulett—can it? There's nothing on earth Paulett can want of me, and he would not come at this hour. Pullet—Pullet—let us see." But he *could* not see, there was not a soul he knew who bore that name.

"He's eating his dinner, sir, the gentleman, sir, in the small parlour, and says you'll know him quite well, sir, when you see him," murmured the butler, "and more—"

"Have you got his card?"

"He said, sir, please, it would be time enough when he had heat his dinner."

"Well, so it will."

And Sir Jekyl drank a glass of claret, and returned to his ruminations.

"So, I shall know Pullet quite well when I see him," mused the Baronet, "and he'll let me have his card when he has had his dinner— a cool gentleman, whatever else he may be." About this Pullet, however, Sir Jekyl experienced a most uncomfortable suspense and curiosity. A bird of ill omen he seemed to him—an angel of sorrow, he knew not why, in a mask.

While the Baronet sipped his claret, and walked quite alone in the midst of his company, picking his anxious steps, and hearing strange sounds through his valley of the shadow of death, the promiscuous assemblage of ladies and gentlemen dissolved itself. The fair sex rose, after their wont, smiled their last on the sable file of gentlemen, who stood politely, napkin in hand, simpering over the backs of their chairs, and, some of them majestically alone, others sliding their fair hands affectionately within the others' arms, glided through the door in celestial procession.

"I shall leave you to-morrow, Sir Jekyl," began the Bishop, gravely, changing his seat to one just vacated beside his host, and bringing with him his principal chattels, his wine-glasses and napkin.

"I do hope, my lord, you'll reconsider that," interrupted Sir Jekyl, laying his fingers kindly on the prelate's purple sleeve. A dismal cloud in Sir Jekyl's atmosphere was just then drifting over him, and he clung, as men do under such shadows, to the contact of good and early friendship.

"I am, I assure you, very sorry, and have enjoyed your hospitality much—*very* much; but we can't rest long, you know: we hold a good many strings, and matters won't wait our convenience."

"I'm only afraid you are overworked; but, of course, I understand how you feel, and shan't press," said Sir Jekyl.

"And I was looking for you to-day in the library," resumed the Bishop, "anxious for a few minutes, on a subject I glanced at when I arrived."

"I—I *know*," said Sir Jekyl, a little hesitatingly.

"Yes, the dying wish of poor Sir Harry Marlowe, your father," murmured the Bishop, looking into his claret-glass, which he slowly turned about by the stem; and, to do him justice, there was not a quarter of a glassful remaining in the bottom.

"I know—to be sure. I quite agree with your lordship's view. I wish to tell you that—quite, I assure you. I don't—I *really* don't at all understand his reasons; but, as you say, it is a case for implicit submission. I intend, I assure you, actually to take down that room during the spring. It is of no real use, and rather spoils the house."

"I am happy, my dear Sir Jekyl, to hear you speak with so much decision on the subject—truly happy;" and the venerable prelate laid his hand with a gentle dignity on the cuff of Sir Jekyl's dress-coat, after the manner of a miniature benediction. "I *may* then discharge *that* quite from my mind?"

"Certainly—quite, my lord. I accept your views implicitly."

"And the *box*—the other wish—you know," murmured the Bishop.

"I must honestly say, I can't the least understand what can have been in my poor father's mind when he told me to—to do what was right with it—was not that it? For I do assure you, for the life of me, I can't think of anything to *be* done with it but let it *alone*. I pledge you my honour, however, if I ever do get the least inkling of his meaning, I will respect it as implicitly as the other."

"Now, now, that's exactly what I wish. I'm perfectly satisfied you'll do what's right."

And as he spoke the Bishop's countenance brightened, and he drank slowly, looking up toward the ceiling, that quarter of a glass of claret on which he had gazed for so long in the bottom of the crystal chalice.

Just then the butler once more inclined his head from the back of Sir Jekyl's chair, and presented a card to his master on the little salver at his left side. It bore the inscription, "Mr. Pelter, Camelia Villa," and across this, perpendicularly, after the manner of a joint "acceptance" of the firm, was written—"Pelter and Crowe, Chambers, Lincoln's Inn Fields," in bold black pencilled lines.

"Why did not you tell me that before?" whispered the Baronet, tartly, half rising, with the card in his hand.

"I was not haware, Sir Jekyl. The gentleman, said his name exactly like Pullet."

"In the library? Well—tell him I'm coming," said Sir Jekyl; and his heart sank, he knew not why.

"Beg your pardon, my lord, for a moment—my man of business, all the way from London, and I fancy in a hurry. I shall get rid of him with a word or two—you'll excuse me? Dives, will you oblige me—

take my place for a moment, and see that the bottle does not stop; or, Doocey, will you?—Dives is doing duty at the foot."

Doocey had hopes that the consultation with the butler portended a bottle of that wonderful Constantia which he had so approved two days before, and took his temporary seat hopefully.

Sir Jekyl, with a general apology and a smile glided away without fuss, and the talk went on much as before.

When the parlour-door shut behind Sir Jekyl, his face darkened. "I know it's some *stupid* thing," he thought, as he walked down the gallery with rapid steps, toward the study, the sharp air agitating, as he did so, his snowy necktie and glossy curls.

"How d'ye do, Mr. Pelter?—very happy to see you. I had not a notion it was you—the stupid fellow gave me quite another name. Quite well, I hope?"

"Quite well, Sir Jekyl, I thank you—a—quite well," said the attorney, a stoutish, short, wealthy-looking man, with a massive gold chain, a resolute countenance, and a bullet head, with close-cut greyish hair.

Pelter was, indeed, an able, pushing fellow, without Latin or even English grammar, having risen in the office from a small clerkship, and, perhaps, was more useful than his gentlemanlike partner.

"Well—a—well, and what has brought you down here? Very glad to see you, you know; but you would not run down for fun, I'm afraid," said Sir Jekyl.

"Au—no—au, well, Sir Jekyl, it has turned out, sir—by gad, sir, I believe them fellows *are* in England, after all!"

"What do you mean by them fellows?" said Sir Jekyl, with a very dark look, unconsciously repeating the attorney's faulty grammar.

"Strangways and Deverell, you know—I mean them—Herbert Strangways, and a young man named Deverell—they're in England,

I've been informed, very private—and Strangways has been with Smith, Rumsey, and Snagg—the office—you know; and there is something on the stocks there."

As the attorney delivered this piece of intelligence he kept his eye shrewdly on Sir Jekyl, rather screwed and wrinkled, as a man looks against a storm.

"Oh!—is that all? There's nothing very alarming, is there, in that?—though, d—— me, I don't see, Mr. Pelter, how you reconcile your present statement with what you and your partner wrote to me twice within the last few weeks."

"Very true, Sir Jekyl; perfectly true, sir. Our information misled us totally; they have been devilish sharp, sir—devilish sly. We never were misled before about that fellow's movements—not that they were ever of any real importance."

"And why do you think them—but maybe you don't—of more consequence now?"

Pelter looked unpleasantly important, and shook his head.

"What *is* it—I suppose I may *know*?" said Sir Jekyl.

"It looks queerish, Sir Jekyl, there's no denying that—in fact, very queerish indeed—both me and my partner think so. You recollect the deed?"

"No—devil a deed—d—— them all!—I don't remember one of them. Why, you seem to forget it's nearly ten years ago," interrupted the Baronet.

"Ah!—no—not *ten*—the copy of the deed that we got hold of, pretending to be a marriage settlement. It was brought us, you know, in a very odd way, but quite fair."

"Yes, I do remember—yes, to be sure—that thing you thought was a forgery, and put in our way to frighten us. Well, and do you fancy that's a genuine thing now?"

"I always thought it might—I think it *may*—in fact, I think it *is*. We have got a hint they rely on it. And here's a point to be noted: the deed fixes five-and-twenty as the period of his majority; and just as he attains that age, his father being nearly that time dead, they put their shoulders to the wheel."

"Put their d—d numbskulls under it, you mean. How can they move—how can they stir? I'd like to know how they can touch my title? I don't care a curse about them. What the plague's frightening you and Crowe *now*? I'm blest if I don't think you're growing old. Why can't you stick to your own view?—you say one thing one day and another the next. Egad, there's no knowing where to have you."

The Baronet was talking bitterly, scornfully, and with all proper contempt of his adversaries, but there's no denying he looked very pale.

"And there certainly is activity there; cases have been with counsel on behalf of Guy Deverell, the son and heir of the deceased," pursued Mr. Pelter, with his hands in his pockets, looking grimly up into the Baronet's face.

"Won't you sit down?—do sit down, Pelter; and you haven't had wine?" said Sir Jekyl.

"Thanks—I've had some sherry."

"Well, you must have some claret. I'd like a glass myself."

He had rung the hell, and a servant appeared.

"Get claret and glasses for two."

The servant vanished deferentially.

"I'm not blaming you, mind; but is it not odd we should have known nothing of this son, and this pretended marriage till now?"

"Odd!—oh dear, no!—you don't often know half so much of the case at the other side—nothing at all often till it's on the file."

"Precious satisfactory!" sneered Sir Jekyl.

"When we beat old Lord Levesham, in Blount and Levesham, they had not a notion, no more than the man in the moon, what we were going on, till we produced the release, and got a direction, egad." And the attorney laughed over that favourite recollection.

CHAPTER XIV.

Pelter opens his mind.

"Take a glass of claret. This is '34. Maybe you'd like some port better?"

"No, thanks, this will do very nicely," said the accommodating attorney. "Thirty-four? So it is, egad! and uncommon fine too."

"I hope you can give me a day or two—not business, of course—I mean by way of holiday," said Sir Jekyl. "A little country air will do you a world of good—set you up for the term."

Mr. Pelter smiled, and shook his head shrewdly.

"Quite out of the question, Sir Jekyl, I thank you all the same—business tumbling in too fast just now—I daren't stay away another day—no, no—ha, ha, ha! no rest for us, sir—no rest for the wicked. But this thing, you know, looks rather queerish, we thought—a little bit urgent: the other party has been so sly; and no want of money, sir—the sinews of war—lots of tin there."

"Yes, of course; and lots of tin here, too. I fancy fellows don't like to waste money only to hold their own; but, egad, if it comes to be a pull at the long purse, all the worse for them," threw in the Baronet.

"And their intending, you know, to set up this marriage," continued the attorney without minding; "and that Herbert Strangways being over here with the young pretender, as we call him, under his wing; and Strangways is a deuced clever fellow, and takes devilish sound view of a case when he lays his mind to it. It was he that reopened that great bankruptcy case of Onslow and Grawley, you remember."

Sir Jekyl assented, but did not remember.

"And a devilish able bit of chess-play that was on both sides—no end of concealed property—brought nearly sixty thousand pounds into the fund, egad! The creditors passed a vote, you remember—spoke very handsomely of him. Monstrous able fellow, egad!"

"A monstrous able fellow he'll be if he gets my property, egad! It seems to me you Pelter and Crowe are half in love with him," said Sir Jekyl, flushed and peevish.

"We'll hit him a hard knock or two yet, for all that—ha, ha!—or I'm mistaken," rejoined old Mr. Pelter.

"Do you know him?" inquired Sir Jekyl; and the servant at the same time appearing in answer to his previous summons, he said—

"Go to the parlour and tell Mr. Doocey—you know *quietly*—that I am detained by business, but that we'll join them in a little time in the drawing-room."

So the servant, with a reverence, departed.

"I say, *do* you?"

"Just a little. Seven years ago, when I was at Havre, he was stopping there too. A very gentlemanlike man—sat beside him twice at the table d'hôte. I could see he knew d—d well who I was—wide awake, very agreeable man, very—wonderful well-informed. Wonderful ups and downs that fellow's had—clever fellow—ha, ha, ha!—I mentioned you, Sir Jekyl; I wanted to hear if he'd say anything—fishing, hey? Old file, you know"—and the attorney winked and grinned agreeably at Sir Jekyl. "Capital claret this—cap-i-tal, by Jupiter! It came in natural enough. We were talking of England, you see. He was asking questions; and so, talking of country gentlemen, and county influence, and parliamentary life, you know, I brought in *you*, and asked him if he knew Sir Jekyl Marlowe." Another wink and a grin here. "I asked, a bit suddenly, you know, to see how he'd take it. Did not show, egad! more than that decanter—ha, ha, ha!—devilish cool dog—monstrous clever fellow—not a bit; and he said he did not know you—had not that honour; but he knew a great deal of you, and he spoke very handsomely—upon my honour—quite au—au—handsomely of you, he did."

"Vastly obliged to him," said Sir Jekyl; but though he sneered I think he was pleased. "You don't recollect what he said, I dare say?"

"Well, I can*not* exactly."

"Did he mention any unpleasantness ever between us?" continued Sir Jekyl.

"Yes, he said there had, and that he was afraid Sir Jekyl might not remember his name with satisfaction; but he, for his part, liked to forget and forgive—that kind of thing, you know, and young fellows being too hot-headed, you know. I really—I don't think he bears you personally any ill-will."

"There has certainly been time enough for anger to cool a little, and I really, for my part, never felt anything of the kind towards him; I can honestly say *that*, and I dare say he knows it. I merely want to protect myself against—against madmen, egad!" said Sir Jekyl.

"I think that copy of a marriage settlement you showed me had no names in it," he resumed.

"No, the case is all put like a moot point, not a name in it. It's all nonsense, too, because every man in my profession knows a copying clerk never has a notion of the meaning of anything—letter, deed, pleading—nothing he copies—not an iota, by Jove!"

"Finish the bottle; you must not send it away," said Sir Jekyl.

"Thanks, I'm doing very nicely; and now as they may open fire suddenly, I want to know"—here the attorney's eyes glanced at the door, and his voice dropped a little—"any information of a confidential sort that may guide us in—in——"

"Why, I fancy it's *all* confidential, isn't it?" answered Sir Jekyl.

"Certainly—but aw—but—I meant—you know—there was aw—a—there was a talk, you know, about a deed. Eh?"

"I—I—*yes*, I've heard—I know what you mean," answered Sir Jekyl, pouring a little claret into his glass. "They—those fellows—they lost a deed, and they were d—d impertinent about it; they wanted—you know it's a long time ago—to try and slur my poor father about it—I don't know exactly how, only, I think, there would have been an action for slander very likely about it, if it had not stopped of itself."

Sir Jekyl sipped his claret.

"I shan't start till three o'clock train to-morrow, if you have anything to say to me," said the attorney, looking darkly and expectingly in Sir Jekyl's face.

"Yes, I'll think over everything. I'd like to have a good talk with you in the morning. You sleep here, you know, of course."

"Very kind. I hope I shan't be in your way, Sir Jekyl. Very happy."

Sir Jekyl rang the bell.

"I shan't let you off to-morrow, unless you really can't help it," he said; and, the servant entering, "Tell Mrs. Sinnott that Mr. Pelter remains here to-night, and would wish—*do* you?—to run up to your room. Where's your luggage?"

"Precious light luggage it is. I left it at the hotel in the town—a small valise, and a——"

"Get it up here, do you mind, and let us know when Mr. Pelter's room is ready."

"Don't be long about dressing; we must join the ladies, you know, in the drawing-room. I wish, Pelter, there was no such thing as business; and that all attorneys, except you and Crowe, of course, were treated in this and the next world according to their deserts," an ambiguous compliment at which Pelter nodded slyly, with his hands in his pockets.

"You'll have to get us all the information you can scrape together, Sir Jekyl. You see they may have evidence of that deed—I mean the lost one, you know—and proving a marriage and the young gentleman legitimate. It may be a serious case—upon my word a *very* serious case—do you see? And term begins, you know, immediately so there really is no time to lose, and there's no harm in being ready."

"I'll have a long talk with you about it in the morning, and I am devilish glad you came—curse the whole thing!"

The servant here came to say that Mr. Pelter's room was ready, and his luggage sent for to the town.

"Come up, then—we'll look at your room."

So up they went, and Pelter declared himself charmed.

"Come to my room, Mr. Pelter—it's a long way off, and a confoundedly shabby crib; but I've got some very good cigars there," said Sir Jekyl, who was restless, and wished to hear the attorney more fully on this hated business.

CHAPTER XV.

The Pipe of Peace.

Sir Jekyl marched Mr. Pelter down the great stair again, intending to make the long journey rearward. As they reached the foot of the stairs, Monsieur Varbarriere, candle in hand, was approaching it on the way to his room. He was walking leisurely, as large men do after dinner, and was still some way off.

"By Jove! Why did not you tell me?" exclaimed the attorney, stopping short. "By the law! you've *got* him here."

"Monsieur Varbarriere?" said the Baronet.

"Mr. Strangways, sir—*that's* he."

"*That* Strangways!" echoed the Baronet.

"Herbert Strangways," whispered Mr. Pelter, and by this time M. Varbarriere was under the rich oak archway, and stopped, smiling darkly, and bowing a little to the Baronet, who was for a moment surprised into silence.

"How do you do, Mr. Strangways, sir?" said the attorney, advancing with a shrewd resolute smile, and extending his hand.

M. Varbarriere, without the slightest embarrassment, took it, bowing with a courtly gravity.

"Ah, Monsieur Pelter?—yes, indeed—very happy to meet you again."

"Yes, sir—very happy, Mr. Strangways; so am I. Did not know you were in this part of the world, Mr. Strangways, sir. You remember Havre, sir?"

"Perfectly—yes. You did not know me by the name of Varbarriere, which name I adopted on purchasing the Varbarriere estates shortly after I met you at Havre, on becoming a naturalised subject of France."

"Wonderful little changed, Monsieur Barvarrian—fat, sir—a little stouter—in good case, Mr. Strangways; but six years, you *know*, sir, does not *count* for *nothing*—ha, ha, ha!"

"You have the goodness to flatter me, I fear," answered Varbarriere, with a smile somewhat contemptuous, and in his deep tones of banter.

"This is my friend, Mr. Strangways, if he'll allow me to call him so—Mr. Herbert Strangways, Sir Jekyl," said the polite attorney, presenting his own guest to the Baronet.

"And so, Monsieur Varbarriere, I find I have an additional reason to rejoice in having made your acquaintance, inasmuch as it revives a very old one, so old that I almost fear you may have forgotten it. You remember our poor friend, Guy Deverell, and—"

"Perfectly, Sir Jekyl, and I was often tempted to ask you the same question; but—but you know there's a *melancholy*—and we were so very happy here, I had not courage to invite the sadness of the retrospect, though a very remote one. I believe I was right, Sir Jekyl. Life's true philosophy is to extract from the present all it can yield of happiness, and to bury our dead out of our sight."

"I dare say—I'm much of that way of thinking myself. And—dear me!—I—I suppose I'm very much altered." He was looking at Varbarriere, and trying to recover in the heavy frame and ponderous features before him the image of that Herbert Strangways whom, in the days of his early coxcombry, he had treated with a becoming impertinence.

"No—you're wonderfully little changed—I say honestly—quite wonderfully like what I remember you. And I—I know what a transformation I am—perfectly," said Varbarriere.

And he stood before Sir Jekyl, as he would display a portrait, full front—Sir Jekyl held a silver candlestick in his hand, Monsieur Varbarriere his in his—and they stood face to face—in a dream of the past.

Varbarriere's mystic smile expanded to a grin, and the grin broke into a laugh—deep and loud—not insulting—not sneering.

In that explosion of sonorous and enigmatic merriment Sir Jekyl joined—perhaps a little hesitatingly and coldly, for he was trying, I think, to read the riddle—wishing to be quite sure that he might be pleased, and accept these vibrations as sounds of reconciliation.

There was nothing quite to forbid it.

"I see," said Monsieur Varbarriere, in tones still disturbed by laughter, "in spite of your politeness, Sir Jekyl, what sort of impression my metamorphosis produces. Where is the raw-boned youth—so tall and gawky, that, egad! London bucks were ashamed to acknowledge him in the street, and when they did speak could not forbear breaking his gawky bones with their jokes?—ha, ha, ha! Now, lo! here he stands—the grand old black swine, on hind legs— hog-backed—and with mighty paunch and face all draped in fat. Bah! ha, ha, ha! What a magician is Father Time! Look and laugh, sir—you cannot laugh more than I."

"I laugh at your fantastic caricature, so utterly unlike what I see. There's a change, it's true, but no more than years usually bring; and, by Jove! I'd much rather any day grow a little full, for *my* part, than turn, like some fellows, into a scarecrow."

"No, no—no scarecrow, certainly," still laughed Varbarriere.

"Egad, no," laughed the attorney in chorus. "No corners there, sir— ribs well covered—hey? nothing like it coming on winter;" and grinning pleasantly, he winked at Sir Jekyl, who somehow neither heard nor saw him, but said—

"Mr. Pelter, my law adviser here, was good enough to say he'd come to my room, which you know so well, Monsieur Varbarriere, and smoke a cigar. You can't do better—pray let me persuade you."

He was in fact tolerably easily persuaded, and the three gentlemen together—Sir Jekyl feeling as if he was walking in a dream, and leading the way affably—reached that snuggery which Varbarriere had visited so often before.

"Just *one*—they *are* so good," said he. "We are to go to the drawing-room—aren't we?"

"Oh, certainly. I think you'll like these—they're rather good, Mr. Pelter. You know them, Monsieur Varbarriere."

"I've hardly ever smoked such tobacco. Once, by a chance, at Lyons, I lighted on a box very like these—that is, about a third of them—but hardly so good."

"We've smoked some of these very pleasantly together," said Sir Jekyl, cultivating genial relations.

Varbarriere, who had already one between his lips, grunted a polite assent with a nod. You would have thought that his whole soul was in his tobacco, as his dark eyes dreamily followed the smoke that thinly streamed from his lips. His mind, however, was busy in conjecturing what the attorney had come about, and how much he knew of his case and his plans. So the three gentlemen puffed away in silence for a time.

"Your nephew, Mr. Guy Strangways, I hope we are soon to see him again?" asked Sir Jekyl, removing his cigar for a moment.

"You are very good. Yes, I hope. In fact, though I call it business, it is only a folly which displeases me, which he has promised shall end; and whenever I choose to shake hands, he will come to my side. There is no real quarrel, mind," and Varbarriere laughed, "only I must cure him of his nonsense."

"Well, then we may hope very soon to see Mr. Strangways. I *call* him Strangways, you know, because he has assumed that name, I suppose, permanently."

"Well, I think so. His real name is Deverell—a very near relation, and, in fact, representative of our poor friend Guy. His friends all thought it best he should drop it, with its sad associations, and assume a name that may be of some little use to him among more affluent relatives," said M. Varbarriere, who had resolved to be frank as day and harmless as doves, and to disarm suspicion adroitly.

"A particularly handsome fellow—a distinguished-looking young man. How many things, Monsieur Varbarriere, we wish undone as we get on in life!"

The attorney lay back in his chair, his hands in his pockets, his heels on the carpet, his cigar pointing up to the ceiling, and his eyes closed luxuriously. He intended making a note of everything.

"I hope to get him on rapidly in the French service," resumed Varbarriere, "and I can make him pretty comfortable myself while I live, and more so after I'm gone; and in the meantime I am glad to put him in a field where he must exert himself, and see something of labour as well as of life."

There was a knock at the door, and the intelligence that Mr. Pelter's luggage was in his room. He would have stayed, perhaps, but Sir Jekyl, smiling, urged haste, and as his cigar was out, he departed. When he was quite gone, Sir Jekyl rose smiling, and extended his hand to Varbarriere, who took it smiling in his own way; also, Sir Jekyl was looking in the face of the large man who stood before him, and returning his gaze a little cloudily; and laughing, both shook hands for a good while, and there was nothing but this low-toned laughter between them.

"At all events, Herbert, I'm glad we have met, very glad—very, very. I did not think I'd have felt it quite this way. I've your forgiveness to ask for a great deal. I never mistook a man so much in my life. I believe you are a devilish good fellow; but—but I fancied, you know, for a long time, that you had taken a hatred to me, and—and I have done you great injustice; and I wish very much I could be of any use to—to that fine young fellow, and show any kindness worth the name towards you."

Sir Jekyl's eyes were moist, he was smiling, and he was shaking Varbarriere's powerful hand very kindly. I cannot analyse his thoughts and feelings in that moment of confusion. It had overcome him suddenly—it had in some strange way even touched Varbarriere. Was there dimly seen by each a kindly solution of a life-long hatred—a possibility of something wise, perhaps self-sacrificing, that led to reconciliation and serenity in old days?

Varbarriere leaned his great shoulders to the wall, his hand still in Sir Jekyl's, still smiling, and looked almost sorrowfully, while he uttered something between a long pant and a sigh.

"Wonderful thing life is—terrible battle, life!" murmured Varbarriere, leaning against the wall, with his dark eyes raised to the far cornice, and looking away and through and beyond it into some far star.

There are times when your wide-awake gentlemen dream a little, and Sir Jekyl laughed a pensive and gentle little laugh, shaking his head and smiling sadly in reply.

"Did you ever read Vathek?" asked the Baronet, "rather a good horror—the fire, you know—ah, ha!—that's a fire every fellow has a spark of in him; I know I have. I've had everything almost a fellow wants; but this I know, if I were sure that death was only rest and darkness, there's hardly a day I live I would not choose it." And with this sentiment came a sincere and odd little laugh.

"My faith! I believe it's true," said Varbarriere with a shrug, and a faint smile of satiety on his heavy features.

"We must talk lots together, Herbert—talk a great deal. You'll find I'm not such a bad fellow after all. Egad, I'm *very* glad you're here!"

CHAPTER XVI.

A Rencontre in the Gallery.

It was time now; however, that they should make their appearance in the drawing-room; so, for the present, Varbarriere departed. He reached his dressing-room in an undefined state—a sort of light, not of battle fires, but of the dawn in his perspective; when, all on a sudden, came the image of a white-moustached, white-browed, grim old military man, glancing with a clear, cold eye, that could be cruel, from the first-class carriage window, up and down the platform of a gas-lit station, some hour and a half away from Slowton, and then sternly at his watch.

"The stupid old fogey!" thought Varbarriere, with a pang, as he revised his toilet hurriedly for the drawing-room. "Could that episode be evaded?"

There was no time to arrive at a clear opinion on this point, nor, indeed, to ascertain very clearly what his own wishes pointed at. So, in a state rather anarchic, he entered the gallery, *en route* for the drawing-room.

Monsieur Varbarriere slid forth, fat and black, from his doorway, with wondrous little noise, his bulk considered, and instantly on his retina, lighted by the lamp at the cross galleries, appeared the figure of a tall thin female, attired in a dark cloak and bonnet, seated against the opposite wall, not many steps away. Its head turned, and he saw Donica Gwynn. It was an odd sort of surprise; he had just been thinking of her.

"Oh! I did not think as you were here, sir; I thought you was in Lunnon."

"Yet here I am, and you too, both unexpectedly." A suspicion had crossed his mind. "How d'ye do, Mrs. Gwynn?"

"Well, I thank you, sir."

"Want *me* here?"

"No, sir; I was wrote for by missus please."

"Yes," he said very slowly, looking hard at her. "Very good, Mrs. Gwynn; have you anything to say to me?"

It would not do, of course, to protract this accidental talk; he did not care to be seen *tête-à-tête* with Donica Gwynn in the gallery.

"No, sir, please, I han't nothing to say, sir," and she courtesied.

"Very well, Mrs. Gwynn; we're quite secret, hey?" and with another hard look, but only momentary, in her face, he proceeded toward the head of the staircase.

"Beg parding, sir, but I think you dropt something." She was pointing to a letter, doubled up, and a triangular corner of which stuck up from the floor, a few yards away.

"Oh! thank you," said Varbarriere, quickly retracing his steps, and picking it up.

A terrible fact for the world to digest is this, that some of our gentlemen attorneys are about the most slobbering men of business to be found within its four corners. They will mislay papers, and even lose them; they are dilatory and indolent—quite the reverse of our sharp, lynx-eyed, energetic notions of that priesthood of Themis, and prone to every sort and description of lay irregularity in matters of order and pink tape.

Our friend Pelter had a first-rate staff, and a clockwork partner beside in Crowe, so that the house was a very regular one, and was himself, in good measure, the fire, bustle, and impetus of the firm. But every virtue has its peccant correspondent. If Pelter was rapid, decided, daring, he was also a little hand-over-hand. He has been seen in a hurry to sweep together and crunch like a snowball a drift of banknotes, and stuff them so impressed into the bottom of his great-coat pocket! What more can one say?

This night, fussing out at his bed-room door, he plucked his scented handkerchief from his pocket, and, as he crossed his threshold, with it flirted forth a letter, which had undergone considerable attrition in that receptacle, and was nothing the whiter, I am bound to admit, especially about the edges, for its long sojourn there.

Varbarriere knew the handwriting and I. M. M. initials in the left-hand lower angle. So, with a nod and a smile, he popped it into his trowsers pocket, being that degree more cautious than Pelter.

Sir Jekyl was once more in high spirits. To do him justice, he had not affected anything. There had been an effervescence—he hardly knew how it came about. But his dangers seemed to be dispersing; and, at the worst, were not negotiation and compromise within his reach?

Samuel Pelter, Esq., gentleman attorney and a solicitor of the High Court of Chancery, like most prosperous men, had a comfortable confidence in himself; and having heard that Lady Alice Redcliffe was quarrelling with her lawyer, thought there could be no harm in his cultivating her acquaintance.

The old lady was sitting in a high-backed chair, very perpendicularly, with several shawls about and around her, stiff and pale; but her dusky eyes peered from their sunken sockets, in grim and isolated observation.

Pelter strutted up. He was not, perhaps, a distinguished-looking man—rather, I fear, the contrary. His face was broad and smirking, with a short, broad, blue chin, and a close crop of iron-grey on his round head, and plenty of crafty crow's-feet and other lines well placed about.

He stood on the hearthrug, within easy earshot of Lady Alice, whom he eyed with a shrewd glance, "taking her measure," as his phrase was, and preparing to fascinate his prey.

"Awful smash that, ma'am, on the Smather and Sham Junction," said Pelter, having fished up a suitable topic. "Frightful thing—fourteen killed—and they say upwards of seventy badly hurt. I'm no chicken, Lady Alice, but by Jove, ma'am, I can't remember any such casualty—a regular ca-tas-trophe, ma'am!"

And Pelter, with much feeling, gently lashed his paunch with his watch-chain and bunch of seals, an obsolete decoration, which he wore—I believe still wears.

Lady Alice, who glowered sternly on him during this speech, nodded abruptly with an inarticulate sound, and then looked to his left, at a distant picture.

"I trust I see you a great deal better, Lady Alice. I have the pleasure, I believe, to address Lady Alice Redcliffe—aw, haw, h'm," and the attorney executed his best bow, a ceremony rather of agility than grace. "I had the honour of seeing you, Lady Alice Redcliffe, at a shower-flow—flower-show, I mean—in the year—let me see— egad, ma'am, twelve—no—no—*thirteen* years ago. How time does fly! Of course all them years—*thirteen*, egad!—has not gone for nothing. I dare say you don't perceive the alterations in yourself— no one does—I wish no one else did—that was always my wish to Mrs. P. of a morning—*my* good lady, Mrs. Pelter—ha, ha, ha! Man can't tether time or tide, as the Psalm says, and every year scribbles a wrinkle or two. You were suffering, I heard then, ma'am, chronic cough, ma'am—and all that. I hope it's abated—I know it will, ma'am—my poor lady is a martyr to it—troublesome thing—very— awful troublesome! Lady Alice."

There was no reply, Lady Alice was still looking sternly at the picture.

"I remember so well, ma'am, you were walking a little lame then, linked with Lord Lumdlebury—(we have had the honour to do business occasionally for his lordship)—and I was informed by a party with me that you had been with Pincendorf. I don't think much of them jockeys, ma'am, for my part; but if it was anything of a callosity—"

Without waiting for any more, Lady Alice Redcliffe rose in solemn silence to her full height, beckoned to Beatrix, and said grimly—

"I'll change my seat, dear, to the sofa—will you help me with these things?"

Lady Alice glided awfully to the sofa, and the gallant Mr. Pelter instituted a playful struggle with Beatrix for possession of the shawls.

"I remember the time, miss, I would not have let you carry your share; but, as I was saying to Lady Alice Redcliffe—"

He was by this time tucking a shawl about her knees, which, so soon as she perceived, she gasped to Beatrix—

"Where's Jekyl?—I can't have *this* any longer—call him here."

"As I was saying to you, Lady Alice, ma'am, our joints grow a bit rusty after sixty; and talking of feet, I passed the Smather and Slam Junction, ma'am, only two hours after the collision; and, egad! there were three feet all in a row cut off by the instep, quite smooth, ma'am, lying in the blood there, a pool as long as the passage up-stairs—awful sight!"

Lady Alice rose up again, with her eyes very wide, and her mouth very close, apparently engaged in mental prayer, and her face angry and pink, and she beckoned with tremulous fingers to Sir Jekyl, who was approaching with one of his provoking smiles.

"I say, Mr. Pelter, my friend Doocey wants you over there; they're at logger-heads about a law point, and I can't help them."

"Hey! if it's *practice* I can give them a wrinkle maybe;" and away stumped the attorney, his fists in his pockets, smirking, to the group indicated by his host.

"Hope I haven't interrupted a conversation? What can I do for you?" said Sir Jekyl, gaily.

"What do you *mean*, Jekyl Marlowe—what *can* you mean by bringing such persons here? What pleasure can you *possibly* find in low and *dreadful* society?—none of your family liked it. Where did you find that man? How on earth did you procure such a person? If I *could*—if I had been well enough, I'd have rung the bell and ordered your servant to remove him. I'd have gone to my bed-room, sir, only that even there I could not have felt safe from his intrusions. It's utterly intolerable and preposterous!"

"I had no idea my venerable friend, Pelter, could have pursued a lady so cruelly; but rely upon me, I'll protect you."

"I think you had better cleanse your house of such persons; at all events, I insist they shan't be allowed to make their horrible sport of me!" said Lady Alice, darting a fiery glance after the agreeable attorney.

CHAPTER XVII.

Old Donnie and Lady Jane.

"Can you tell me, child, anything about that horrible fat old Frenchman, who has begun to speak English since his return?" asked Lady Jane Lennox of Beatrix, whom she stopped, just touching her arm with the tip of her finger, as she was passing. Lady Jane was leaning back indolently, and watching the movements of M. Varbarriere with a disagreeable interest.

"That's Monsieur Varbarriere," answered Beatrix.

"Yes, I know that; but who is he—what is he? I wish he were gone," replied she.

"I really know nothing of him," replied Beatrix, with a smile.

"Yes, you do know something about him: for instance, you know he's the uncle of that handsome young man who accompanied him." This Lady Jane spoke with a point which caused on a sudden a beautiful scarlet to tinge the young girl's cheeks.

Lady Jane looked at her, without a smile, without archness, with a lowering curiosity and something of pain, one might fancy, even of malignity.

Lady Jane hooked her finger in Beatrix's bracelet, and lowering her eyes to the carpet, remained silent, it seemed to the girl undecided whether to speak or not on some doubtful subject. With a vague interest Beatrix watched her handsome but sombre countenance, till Lady Jane appearing to escape from her thoughts, with a little toss of her beautiful head and a frown, said, looking up—

"Beatrix, I have such frightful dreams sometimes. I am ill, I think; I am horribly nervous to-night."

"Would you like to go to your room? Maybe if you were to lie down, Lady Jane—"

"By-and-by, perhaps—yes." She was still stealthily watching Varbarriere.

"I'll go with you—shall I?" said Beatrix.

"No, you shan't," answered Lady Jane, rudely.

"And why, Lady Jane?" asked Beatrix, hurt and surprised.

"You shall never visit my room; you are a good little creature. I could have loved you, Beatrix, but now I can't."

"Yet I like you, and you meet me so! why is this?" pleaded Beatrix.

"I can't say, little fool; who ever knows why they like or dislike? I don't. The fault, I suppose, is mine, not yours. I never said it was yours. If you were ever so little wicked," she added, with a strange little laugh, "perhaps I could; but it is not worth talking about," and with a sudden change from this sinister levity to a seriousness which oscillated strangely between cruelty and sadness, she said—

"Beatrix, you like that young man, Mr. Strangways?" Again poor Beatrix blushed, and was about to falter an exculpation and a protest; but Lady Jane silenced it with a grave and resolute "*Yes—you like him*;" and after a little pause, she added—"Well, if you don't marry *him*, marry no one else;" and shortly after this, Lady Jane sighed heavily.

This speech of hers was delivered in a way that prevented evasion or girlish hypocrisy, and Beatrix had no answer but that blush which became her so; and dropping her eyes to the ground, she fell into a reverie, from which she was called up by Lady Jane, who said suddenly—

"What can that fat Monsieur Varbarriere be? He looks like Torquemada, the Inquisitor—mysterious, plausible, truculent—what do you think? Don't you fancy he could poison you in an ice or a cup of coffee; or put you into Cardinal Ballue's cage, and smile on you once a year through the bars?"

Beatrix smiled, and looked on the unctuous old gentleman with an indulgent eye, comparatively.

"I can't see him so melodramatically, Lady Jane," she laughed. "To me he seems a much more commonplace individual, a great deal less interesting and atrocious, and less like the abbot."

"What abbot?" said Lady Jane, sharply, "Now really that's very odd."

"I meant," said Beatrix, laughing, "the Abbot of Quedlinberg, in Canning's play, who is described, you know, as very corpulent and cruel."

"Oh, I forgot; I don't think I ever read it; but it chimed in so oddly with my dreams."

"How, what do you mean?" cried Beatrix, amused.

"I dreamed some one knocked at night at my door, and when I said 'come in,' that Monsieur Varbarriere put in his great face, with a hood on like a friar's, smiling like—like an assassin; and somehow I have felt a disgust of him ever since."

"Well, I really think he would look rather well in a friar's frock and hood," said Beatrix, glancing at the solemn old man again with a little laugh. "He would do very well for Mrs. Radcliff's one-handed monk, or Schedone, or some of those awful ecclesiastics that scare us in books."

"I think him positively odious, and I hate him," said Lady Jane, quietly rising. "I mean to steal away—will you come with me to the foot of the stair?"

"Come," whispered Beatrix; and as Lady Jane lighted her candle, in that arched recess near the foot of the stair, where, in burnished silver, stand the files of candles, awaiting the fingers which are to bear them off to witness the confidences of toilet or of dejection, she said—

"Well, as you won't take me with you, we must part here. Good-night, Lady Jane."

Lady Jane turned as if to kiss her, but only patted her on the cheek, and said coldly—

"Good-bye, little fool—now run back again."

When Lady Jane reached the gallery at the top of the staircase, she, too, saw Donica Gwynn seated where Varbarriere had spoken to her.

"Ha! Donica," cried she suddenly, in the accents of early girlhood, "I'm so glad to see you, Donica. You hardly know me now?"

And Lady Jane, in the light of one transient, happy smile, threw her jewelled arms round the neck of the old housekeeper, whose visits of weeks at a time to Wardlock were nearly her happiest remembrances of that staid old mansion.

"You dear old thing! you were always good to me; and I such a madcap and such a fury! Dull enough now, Donnie, but not a bit better."

"My poor Miss Jennie!" said old Donica Gwynn, with a tender little laugh, her head just a little on one side, looking on her old pet and charge with such a beautiful, soft lighting up of love in her hard old face as you would not have fancied could have beamed there. Oh! most pathetic mystery, how in our poor nature, layer over layer, the angelic and the evil, the mean and the noble, lie alternated. How sometimes, at long intervals, in the wintriest life and darkest face, the love of angels will suddenly beam out, and show you, still unwrecked, the eternal capacity for heaven.

"And grown such a fine 'oman—bless ye—I allays said she would—didn't I?"

"You always stood up for me, old Donnie Don. Come into my room with me now, and talk. Yes—come, and talk, and talk, and talk—I have no one, Bonnie, to talk with now. If I had I might be different— I mean better. You remember poor mamma, Donnie—don't you?"

"*Dear!* to be sure—yes, and a nice creature, and a pretty—there's a look in your face sometimes reminds me on her, Miss Jennie. And I allays said you'd do well—didn't I?—and see what a great match, they tell me, you a' made! Well well! and how you *have* grown!—a fine lady, bless you," and she laughed so softly over those thin, girlish images of memory, you'd have said the laugh was as far away and as sad as the remembrance.

"Sit down, Donnie Don," she said, when they had entered the room. "Sit down, and tell me everything—how all the old people are, and how the old place looks—you live there now? *I* have nothing to tell, only I'm married, as you know—and—and I think a most good-for-nothing creature."

"Ah, no, pretty Miss Jane, there was good in you always, only a little bit hasty, and *that* anyone as had the patience could see; and I knowed well you'd be better o' that little folly in time."

"I'm not better, Donnie—I'm worse—I *am* worse, Donnie. I know I am—not better."

"Well, dear! and jewels, and riches, and coaches, and a fine gentleman adoring you—not very young, though. Well, maybe all the better. Did you never hear say, it's better to be an old man's darling than a young man's slave?"

"Yes, Donnie, it's very well; but let us talk of Wardlock—and he's *not* a fine man, Donnie, who put that in your head—he's old, and ugly, and"—she was going to say stupid, but the momentary bitterness was rebuked by an accidental glimpse of the casket in which his splendid present was secured—"and tell me about Wardlock, and the people—is old Thomas Jones there still?"

"No, he's living at Glastonhowe now, with his grandson that's married—very happy; but you would not believe how old he looks, and they say can't remember nothink as he used to, but very comfortable."

"And Turpin, the gardener?"

"Old Turpin be dead, miss, two years agone; had a fit a few months before, poor old fellow, and never was strong after. Very deaf he was of late years, and a bit cross sometimes about the vegetables, they do say; but he was a good-natured fellow, and decent allays; and though he liked a mug of ale, poor fellow, now and then, he was very regular at church."

"Poor old Turpin dead! I never heard it—and *old*? he used to wear a kind of flaxen wig."

"Old! dearie me, that he was, miss, you would not guess how old—there's eighty-five years on the grave-stone that Lady Alice put over him, from the parish register, in Wardlock churchyard, bless ye!"

"And—and as I said just now about my husband, General Lennox, that he was old—well, he *is* old, but he's a good man, and kind, and such a gentleman."

"And you love him—and what more is needed to make you both happy?" added Donica; "and glad I am, miss, to see you so comfortably married—and such a nice, good, grand gentleman; and don't let them young chaps be coming about you with their compliments, and fine talk, and love-making."

"What do you mean, woman? I should hope I know how to behave myself as well as ever Lady Alice Redcliffe did. It is *she* who has been talking to you, and, I suppose, to every one, the stupid, wicked hag."

"Oh, Miss Jennie, dear!"

CHAPTER XVIII.

Alone—Yet not alone.

"Well, Donnie, don't talk about *her*; talk about Wardlock, and the people, and the garden, and the trees, and old Wardlock church," said Lady Jane, subsiding almost as suddenly as she flamed up. "Do you remember the brass tablet about Eleanor Faukes, well-beloved and godly, who died in her twenty-second year, in the year of grace sixteen hundred and thirty-four? See how I remember it! Poor Eleanor Faukes! I often think of her—and do you remember how you used to make me read the two lines at the end of the epitaph? 'What you are I was; what I am you shall be.' Do you remember?"

"Ay, miss, that I do. I wish I could think o' them sorts o' things allays—it's very good, miss."

"Perhaps it is, Donnie. It's very sad and very horrible, at all events, death and judgment," answered Lady Jane.

"Have you your old Bible yet, miss?"

"Not here," answered Lady Jane, colouring a little; but recollecting, she said, "I *have* got a very pretty one, though," and she produced a beautiful volume bound in velvet and gold.

"A deal handsomer, Miss Jennie, but not so well read, I'm afeared," said Donica Gwynn, looking at the fresh binding and shining gilt leaves.

"There it is, Donnie Don; but I feel like you, and I *do* like the old one best, blurred and battered; poor old thing, it looked friendly, and this like a fashionable chaplain. I have not seen it for a long time, Donnie; perhaps it's lost, and this is only a show one, as you see."

And after a few seconds she added, a little bitterly, almost angrily, "I never read my Bible now. I never open it," and then came an unnatural little laugh.

"Oh! Miss Jennie, dear—I mean my Lady Jane—don't say that, darling—*that* way, anyhow, don't say it. Why should not you read your Bible, and love it, better now nor ever, miss—the longer you live the more you'll want it, and when sorrow comes, what have you but that?"

"It's all denunciation, all hard names, and threats, Donnie. If people believed themselves what they *say* every Sunday in church, miserable sinners, and I dare say they are, they'd sicken and quake at sight of it. I hope I may come to like it some day, Donnie," she added, with a short sigh.

"I mind, Miss Jennie—I mean my Lady Jane."

"No, you're to call me Jennie still, or I'll drop Donnie Don, and call you Mrs. Gwynn," said Lady Jane, with her hands on Donica's thin shoulders, playfully, but with a very pensive face and tone.

Donica smiled for a moment, and then her face saddened too, and she said—

"And I mind, Miss Jennie, when it was the same way with me, only with better reason, for I was older than you, and had lived longer than ever you did without a thought of God; but I tell you, miss, you'll find your only comfort there at last; it is not much, maybe, to the like o' me, that can't lay her mind down to it, but it's *some*think; ay, I mind the time I durst not open it, thinking I'd only meet summat there to vex me. But 'tisn't so: there's a deal o' good nature in the Bible, and ye'll be sure to stumble on somethink kind whenever you open it."

Lady Jane made no answer. She looked down with a careworn gaze on her white hand, the fleeting tenement of clay; jewelled rings glimmered on its fingers—the vanities of the world, and under it lay the Bible, the eternal word. She was patting the volume with a little movement that made the brilliants flash. You would have thought she was admiring her rings, but that her eyes were so sad and her gaze so dreamy.

"And I hear the mistress, Lady Alice, a-coming up—yes, 'tis her voice. Good-night, Miss Jennie, dear."

"Good-night, dear old Donnie."

"And you'll promise me you'll read a bit in it every night."

"Where's the use in promising, Donnie? Don't we promise everything—the whole Christian religion, at our baptism—and how do we keep it?"

"You must promise you'll read, if 'twas only a verse every night, Miss Jennie, dear—it may be the makin' o' ye. I hear Lady Alice a-calling."

"You're a good old thing—I like you, Donnie—you'd like to make me better—happier, that is—and I love you—and I promise for this night, at all events, I will read a verse, and maybe more, if it turns out good-natured, as you say. Good-night."

And she shook old Gwynn by both hands, and kissed her; and as she parted with her, said—

"And, Donnie, you must tell my maid I shan't want her to-night—and I *will* read, Donnie—and now, good-night again."

So handsome Lady Jane was alone.

"It seems to me as if I had not time to think—God help me, God help me," said Lady Jane. "Shall I read it? That odious book, that puts impossibilities before us, and calls eternal damnation eternal justice!"

"Good-night, Jane," croaked Lady Alice's voice, and the key turned in the door.

With a pallid glance from the corners of her eyes, of intense contempt—*hatred*, even, at the moment, she gazed on the door, as she sate with her fingers under her chin; and if a look could have pierced the panels, hers would have shot old Lady Alice dead at the other side. For about a minute she sat so, and then a chilly little laugh rang from her lips; and she thought no more for a while of Lady Alice, and her eyes wandered again to her Bible.

"Yes, that odious book! with just power enough to distract us, without convincing—to embitter our short existence, without directing it; I *hate* it."

So she said, and looked as if she would have flung it into the farthest corner of the room. She was spited with it, as so many others are, because it won't do for us what we must do for ourselves.

"When sorrow comes, poor Donnie says—*when* it comes—little she knows how long it has been here! Life—such a dream—such an agony often. Surely it pays the penalty of all its follies. Judgment indeed! The all-wise Creator sitting in judgment upon creatures like us, living but an hour, and walking in a dream!"

This kind of talk with her, as with many others, was only the expression of a form of pain. She was perhaps in the very mood to read, that is, with the keen and anxious interest that accompanies and indicates a deep-seated grief and fear.

It was quite true what she said to old Donica. These pages had long been sealed for her. And now, with a mixture of sad antipathy and interest, as one looks into a coffin, she did open the book, and read here and there in a desultory way, and then, leaning on her hand, she mused dismally; then made search for a place she wanted, and read and wept, wept aloud and long and bitterly.

The woman taken, and "set in the midst," the dreadful Pharisees standing round. The Lord of life, who will judge us on the last day, hearing and *saving*! Oh, blessed Prince, whose service is perfect freedom, how wise are thy statutes! "More to be desired are they than gold—*sweeter* also than honey." Standing between thy poor tempted creatures and the worst sorrow that can befall them—a sorrow that softens, not like others, as death approaches, but is transformed, and stands like a giant at the bedside. May they see thy interposing image—may they see thy face now and for ever.

Rest for the heavy-laden! The broken and the contrite he will not despise. Read and take comfort, how he dealt with that poor sinner. Perfect purity, perfect mercy. Oh, noblest vision that ever rose before contrite frailty! Lift up the downcast head—let the poor heart break no more—you shall rise from the dust an angel.

Suddenly she lifted up her pale face, with an agony and a light on her countenance, with hands clasped, and such a look from the abyss, in her upturned eyes.

Oh! was it possible—could it be true? A *friend*—such a *friend*!

Then came a burst of prayer—wild resolutions—agonised tears. She knew that in all space, for her, was but one place of safety—to lie at the wounded feet of her Saviour, to clasp them, to bathe them with her tears. An hour—more—passed in this agony of stormy hope breaking in gleams through despair. Prayer—cries for help, as from the drowning, and vows frantic—holy, for the future.

"Yes, once more, thank God, I can dare with safety—here and now—to see him for the last time. In the morning I will conjure old Lady Alice to take me to Wardlock. I will write to London. Arthur will join me there. I'd like to go abroad—never into the world again—never—never—never. He will be pleased. I'll try to make amends. He'll never know what a wretch I've been. But he shall see the change, and be happier. Yes, yes, yes." Her beautiful long hair was loose, its rich folds clasped in her strained fingers—her pale upturned face bathed in tears and quivering—"The Saviour's feet!—No happiness but there—wash them with my tears—dry them with this hair." And she lifted up her eyes and hands to heaven.

Poor thing! In the storm, as cloud and rack fly by, the momentary gleam that comes—what is it? Do not often these agitations subside in darkness? Was this to be a lasting sunshine, though saddened for her? Was she indeed safe now and for ever?

But is there any promise that repentance shall arrest the course of the avenger that follows sin on earth? Are broken health or blighted fame restored when the wicked man "turneth away from the wickedness that he hath committed;" and do those consequences that dog iniquity with "feet of wool and hands of iron," stay their sightless and soundless march so soon as he begins to do "that which is lawful and right?" It is enough for him to know that he that does so "shall save his soul alive."

CHAPTER XIX.

Varbarriere the Tyrant debates with the weaker Varbarrieres.

"May I see you, Monsieur Varbarriere, to-morrow, in the room in which I saw you to-day, at any hour you please after half-past eleven?" inquired Lady Alice, a few minutes after that gentleman had approached her.

"Certainly, madam; perhaps I can at this moment answer you upon points which cause you anxiety; pray command me."

And he sate like a corpulent penitent on a low prie-dieu chair beside her knee, and inclined his ear to listen.

"It is only to learn whether my—my poor boy's son, my grandson, the young man in whom I must feel so deep an interest, is about to return here?"

"I can't be quite certain, madam, of that; but I can promise that he will do himself the honour to present himself before you, whenever you may please to appoint, at your house of Wardlock."

"Yes, that would be better still. He could come there and see his old grandmother. I would like to see him soon. I have a great deal to say to him, a great deal to tell him that would interest him; and the pictures; I know you will let him come. Do you really mean it, Monsieur Varbarriere?"

M. Varbarriere smiled a little contemptuously, and bowed most deferentially.

"Certainly madam, I mean what I say; and if I did *not* mean it, still I would say I do."

There was something mazy in this sentence which a little bewildered old Lady Alice's head, and she gazed on Varbarriere with a lack-lustre frown.

"Well, then, sir, the upshot of the matter is that *I may* rely on what you say, and expect my grandson's visit at Wardlock?"

"Certainly, madam, you *may* expect it," rejoined Varbarriere, oracularly.

"And pray, Monsieur Varbarriere, are you married?" inquired the old lady, with the air of a person who had a right to be informed.

"Alas, madam, may I say Latin?—Infandum, regina, jubes renovare dolorem; you stir up my deepest grief. I am, indeed, what you call an old bachelor."

"Well, so I should suppose; I don't see what business you would have had to marry."

"Nor I either," he replied.

"And you are very rich, I suppose."

"The rich man never says he is rich, and the poor man never says he is poor. What shall I say? Pretty well! Will that do?"

"H'm, yes; you ought to make a settlement, Monsieur Varbarriere."

"On your grandson, madam?"

"Yes, my grandson, he's nothing the worse of that, sir—and your nephew."

"Madam, the idea is beneficent, and does honour to your heart. I have, to say truth, had an idea of doing something for him by my will, though not by settlement; you are quite in advance of me, madam—I shall reflect."

Monsieur Varbarriere was, after his wont, gravely amusing himself, so gravely that old Lady Alice never suspected an irony. Old Lady

Alice had in her turn taken up the idea of a solution of all family variance, by a union between Guy Deverell and Beatrix, and her old brain was already at the settlements.

"Lady Alice, you must positively give us up our partner, Monsieur Varbarriere, our game is arrested; and, egad, Pelter, poor fellow, is bursting with jealousy!"

Lady Alice turned disdainfully from Sir Jekyl.

"Monsieur Varbarriere, pray don't allow me to detain you now. I should be very glad to see you, if you had no particular objection, to-morrow."

"Only too happy; you do me, madam, a great deal of honour;" and with a bow and a smile Monsieur Varbarriere withdrew to the whist-table.

He did not play that night by any means so well as usual. Doocey, who was his partner, was, to say the least, disappointed, and Sir Jekyl and Sir Paul made a very nice thing of it, in that small way which makes domestic whist-players happy and serene. When they wound up, Doocey was as much irritated as a perfectly well-bred gentleman could be.

"Well, Sir Paul; we earned our winnings, eh? Four times the trick against honours, not bad play, I think," said Sir Jekyl, as they rose.

"Captain Doocey thinks our play had nothing to do with it," observed Sir Paul, with a faint radiance of complacent banter over his bluff face, as he put his adversary's half-crowns into his trowsers pocket.

"I never said *that*, Sir Paul, of course; you mistake me, but *we* might, don't you think, Monsieur Varbarriere, have played a little better? for instance, we should have played our queen to the lead of spades. I'm sure that would have given us the trick, don't you see, and you would have had the lead, and played diamonds, and forced Sir Jekyl to ruff with his ace, and made my knave good, and that would have given us the lead and trick."

"Our play goes for nothing, you see, Sir Paul," said Sir Jekyl.

"No; Captain Doocey thinks play had nothing to do with it," said Sir Paul Blunket.

"'Gad, I think play had everything to do with it—not *yours*, though," said Doocey, a little tartly.

"I must do you *all* justice," interposed Varbarriere, "you're all right—everyone played well except me. I do pretty well when I'm in the vein, but I'm not to-night; it was a very bad performance. I played execrably, Captain Doocey."

"Oh! no, I won't allow that; but you know once or twice you certainly did not play according to your own principles, I mean, and I couldn't therefore see exactly what you meant, and I dare say it was as much my fault as yours."

And Doocey, with his finger on Varbarriere's sleeve, fell into one of those *resumés* which mysteriously interest whist-players, and Varbarriere listened to his energetic periods with his hands in his pockets, benignant but bored, and assented with a good grace to his own condemnation. And smothering a yawn as he moved away, again pleaded guilty to all the counts, and threw himself on the mercy of the court.

"What shall we do to-morrow?" exclaimed Sir Jekyl, and he heard a voice repeat "to-morrow," and so did Varbarriere. "I'll turn it over, and at breakfast I'll lay half a dozen plans before you, and you shall select. It's a clear frosty night; we shall have a fine day. You don't leave us, Mr. Pelter, till the afternoon, d'ye see? and mind, Lady Alice Redcliffe sits in the boudoir, at the first landing on the great stair; the servant will show you the way; don't fail to pay her a visit, d'ye mind, Pelter; she's huffed, you left her so suddenly; don't mind her at first; just amuse her a little, and I think she's going to change her lawyer."

Pelter, with his hands in his pockets, smiled shrewdly and winked on Sir Jekyl.

"Thanks; I know it, I heard it; you can give us a lift in that quarter, Sir Jekyl, and I shan't forget to pay my respects."

When the ladies had gone, and the gentlemen stood in groups by the fire, or sat listless before it, Sir Jekyl, smiling, laid his hand on Varbarriere's shoulder, and asked him in a low tone—

"Will you join Pelter in my room, and wind up with a cigar?"

"I was going, that is, tempted, only ten minutes ago, to ask leave to join your party," began Varbarriere.

"It is not a party—we should be only three," said Sir Jekyl, in an eager whisper.

"All the more inviting," continued Varbarriere, smiling. "But I suddenly recollected that I shall have rather a busy hour or two— three or four letters to write. My people of business in France never give me a moment; they won't pay my rent or cork a bottle, my faith! without a letter."

"Well, I'm sorry you can't; but you must make it up to me, and see, you must take two or three of these to your dressing-room," and he presented his case to M. Varbarriere.

"Ha! you are very good; but, *no*; I like to connect them with your room, they must not grow too common, they shall remain a treat. No, no, I won't; ha, ha, ha! Thank you very much," and he waved them off, laughing and shaking his head.

Somehow he could not brook accepting this trifling present. To be sure, here he was a guest at free quarters, but at this he stuck; he drew back and waved away the cigar-case. It was not logical, but he could not help it.

When Pelter and Sir Jekyl sat in the Baronet's chamber, under their canopy of tobacco-smoke over their last cigar,

"See, Pelter," said Sir Jekyl, "it won't do to *seem* anxious; the fact is I'm *not* anxious; I believe he has a lot of money to leave that young fellow. Suppose they marry; the Deverells are a capital old family, don't you see, and it will make up everything, and stop people talking about—about old nonsense. I'll settle all, and I don't care a curse, and I'll not be very long in the way. I can't keep always young, I'm past fifty."

"Judging by his manner, you know, I should say any proposition you may have to make he'd be happy to listen to," said Mr. Pelter.

"You're sleepy, Pelter."

"Well, a little bit," said the attorney, blinking, yawning, and grinning all together.

"And, egad, I think you want to be shaved," said Sir Jekyl, who did not stand on ceremony with his attorney.

"Should not wonder," said Mr. Pelter, feeling his chin over sleepily with his finger and thumb. "My shave was at half-past four, and what is it now?—half-past eleven, egad! I thought it was later. Good-night, Sir Jekyl—those *are* cigars, magnificent, by Jove!—and about that Strangways' business, I would not be in too great a hurry, do you see? I would not open anything, till I saw whether they were going to move, or whether there was anything in it. I would not put it in his head, d'ye see, hey?" and from habit Pelter winked.

And with that salutation, harmless as the kiss apostolic, Mr. Pelter, aided by a few directions from Sir Jekyl, toddled away to his bedchamber yawning, and the Baronet, after his wont, locked himself into his room in very tolerable spirits.

There was a sofa in Varbarriere's dressing-room, on which by this time, in a great shawl dressing-gown, supine lay our friend; like the painted stone monument of the Chief Justice of Chester in Wardlock church, you could see on the wall sharply defined in shadow the solemn outline of his paunch. He was thinking—not as we endeavour to trace thought in narrative, like a speech, but crossing zigzag from point to point, and back and forward. A man requires an audience, and pen and paper, to think in train at all. His ideas whisked and jolted on somewhat in this fashion:—

"It is to be *avoided*, if possible. My faith! it is now just twelve o'clock! A dangerous old block-head. I must avoid it, if only for time to think in. There was nothing this evening to imply such relations— Parbleu! a pleasant situation if it prove all a mistake. These atrabilious countrymen and women of mine are so odd, they may mislead a fellow accustomed like me to a more intriguing race and a higher *finesse*. Ah! no; it is certainly true. The *fracas* will end everything. That old white monkey will be sure to blunder me into it. Better reconsider things, and wait. What shall I tell him? No excuse, I must go through with it, or I suppose he will call for pistols—curse him! I'll give Sir Jekyl a hint or two. He must see her, and make all ready. The old fool will blaze away at me, of course. Well! I shall fight him or not, as I may be moved. No one in this country need fight now who does not wish it. Rather a comfortable place to live in, if it were not for the climate. I forgot to ask Jacques whether Guy took all his luggage! What o'clock now? Come, by my faith! it is time to decide."

CHAPTER XX.

M. Varbarriere decides.

Varbarriere sat up on the side of his sofa.

"Who brought that woman, Gwynn, here? What do they want of her?" It was only the formula by which interrogatively to express the suspicion that pointed at Sir Jekyl and his attorney. "Soft words for me while tampering with my witnesses, then laugh at me. Why did not I ask Lady Alice whether she really wrote for her?"

Thus were his thoughts various as the ingredients of that soup called harlequin, which figures at low French taverns, in which are floating bits of chicken, cheese, potato, fish, sausage, and so forth—the flavour of the soup itself is consistent, nevertheless. The tone of Varbarriere's ruminations, on the whole, was decided. He wished to avert the exposure which his interference alone had invited.

He looked at his watch—he had still a little more than half an hour for remedial thought and action—and now, what is to be done to prevent *ce vieux singe blanc* from walking into the green chamber, and keeping watch and ward at his wife's bedside until that spectre shall emerge through the wall, whom with a curse and a stab he was to lay?

Well, what precise measures were to be taken? First he must knock up Sir Jekyl in his room, and tell him positively that General Lennox was to be at Marlowe by one o'clock, having heard stories in town, for the purpose of surprising and punishing the guilty. Sir Jekyl would be sharp enough to warn Lady Jane; or should he suggest that it would be right to let her know, in order to prevent her from being alarmed at the temper and melodramatics of her husband, and to secure that coolness and preparation which were necessary? It required some delicacy and tact, but he was not afraid. Next, he must meet General Lennox, and tell him in substance that he had begun to hope that he had been himself practised upon. Yes, that would do—and he might be as dark as he pleased on the subject of his information.

Varbarriere lighted his bed-room candle, intending to march forthwith to Sir Jekyl's remote chamber.

Great events, as we all know, turn sometimes upon small pivots. Before he set out, he stood for a moment with his candle in one hand, and in his reverie he thrust the other into the pocket of his voluminous black trowsers, and there it encountered, unexpectedly, the letter he had that evening picked up on the floor of the gallery. It had quite dropped out of his mind. Monsieur Varbarriere was a Jupiter Scapin. He had not the smallest scruple about reading it, and afterwards throwing it into the fire, though it contained other men's secrets, and was another man's property.

This was a letter from Sir Jekyl Marlowe to Pelter and Crowe, and was in fact upon the special subject of Herbert Strangways. Unlucky subject! unlucky composition! Now there was, of course, here a great deal of that sort of communication which occurs between a clever attorney and his clever client, which is termed "privileged," and is not always quite fit to see the light. Did ever beauty read letter of compliment and adoration with keener absorption?

Varbarriere's face rather whitened as he read, and his fat sneer was not pleasant to see.

He got through it, and re-commenced. Sometimes he muttered and sometimes he thought; and the notes of this oration would have read nearly thus:—

"So the question is to be opened whether the *anonymous payment*— he lies, it was in *my name*!—through the bankers protects me technically from pursuit; and I'm to be 'run by the old Hebrew pack from cover to cover,' over the Continent—bravo!—till I vanish for seven years more." Here Monsieur Varbarriere laughed in lurid contempt.

The letter went on in the same vein—contemptuous, cruel, he fancied. Everyone *is* cruel in self-defence; and in its allusions and spirit was something which bitterly recalled the sufferings which in younger and weaker days that same Baronet, pursuing the same policy, had inflicted upon him. Varbarriere remembered when he was driven to the most ignominious and risky shifts, to ridiculous disguises; he remembered his image in the cracked shaving-glass in the garret in his lair near Notre Dame—the red wig and moustache, and the goggles.

How easily an incautious poke will re-awake the dormant neuralgia of toothache; and tooth, cheek, ear, throat, brain, are all throbbing again in the re-induced anguish! With these sharp and vivid recollections of humiliation, fear, and suffering, all stirred into activity by this unlucky letter, that savage and vindictive feeling which had for so long ruled the life of Herbert Strangways, and had sunk into an uneasy doze under the narcotic of this evening's interview, rose up suddenly, wide awake and energetic.

He looked at his watch. The minute-hand showed him exactly how long he had been reading this confidence of client to attorney. "You will, will you?" murmured Varbarriere, with his jaw a little fiercely set, and a smile. "He will *checkmate* me, he thinks, in two or three moves. He does not see, clever fellow, that I will checkmate him in *one*!"

Now, this letter had *preceded* all that had occurred this evening to soften old animosities—though, strictly examined, that was not very much. It did not seem quite logical then, that it should work so sudden a revolution. I cannot, however, say positively; for in Varbarriere's mind may have long lain a suspicion that Sir Jekyl was not now altogether what he used to be, that he did not quite know all he had inflicted, and that time had made him wiser, and therefore gentler of heart. If so, the letter had knocked down this hypothesis, and its phrases, one or two of them, were of that unlucky sort which not only recalled the thrill of many an old wound, but freshly galled that vanity which never leaves us, till ear and eye grow cold, and light and sound are shut out by the coffin-lid.

So Varbarriere, being quite disenchanted, wondered at his own illusions, and sighed bitterly when he thought what a fool he had been so near making of himself. And thinking of these things, he stared grimly on his watch, and by one of those movements that betray one's abstraction, held it to his ear, as if he had fancied it might have gone down.

There it was, thundering on at a gallop. The tread of unseen fate approaching. Yes, it was time he should go. Jacques peeped in.

"You've done as I ordered?"

"Yes Monsieur."

"Here, lend me a hand with my cloak—very good. The servants, the butler, have they retired?"

"So I believe, Monsieur."

"My hat—thanks. The lights all out on the stairs and lobbies?"

"Yes, Monsieur."

"Go before—is that lighted?"

"Yes, sir."

This referred to one of those little black lanterns which belong to Spanish melodrama, with a semi-cylindrical horn and a black slide. We have most of us seen such, and handled if not possessed them.

"Leporello! hey, Jacques?" smiled Varbarriere sardonically, as he drew his short black cloak about him.

"Monsieur is always right," acquiesced the man, who had never heard of Leporello before.

"Get on, then."

And the valet before, the master following, treading cautiously, they reached the stair-head, where Varbarriere listened for a moment, then descended and listened again at the foot, and so through the hall into the long gallery, near the end of which is a room with a conservatory.

This they entered. The useful Jacques had secured the key of the glass door into the conservatory, which also opened the outer one; and Varbarriere, directing him to wait there quietly till his return, stepped out into the open air and faint moonlight. A moment's survey was enough to give him the lie of the ground, and recognising the file of tufted lime-trees, rising dark in the mist, he directed his steps thither, and speedily got upon the broad avenue, bordered with grass and guarded at either side by these rows of giant limes.

On reaching the carriage-way, standing upon a slight eminence, Varbarriere gazed down the misty slope toward the gate-house, and then toward Marlowe Manor, in search of a carriage or a human figure. Seeing none, he strolled onward toward the gate, and soon *did* see, airy and faint in the haze and distance, a vehicle approaching. It stopped some two hundred yards nearer the gate than he, a slight figure got out, and after a few words apparently, the driver turned about, and the slim, erect figure came gliding stiffly along in his direction. As he approached Varbarriere stood directly before him.

"Ha! here I am waiting, General," said Varbarriere, advancing. "I— I suppose we had better get on at once to the house?"

General Lennox met him with a nod.

"Don't care, sir. Whatever you think best," answered the General, as sternly as if he were going into action.

"Thanks for your confidence, General. I think so;" and side by side they walked in silence for a while toward the house.

"Lady Alice Redcliffe here?"

"Yes, sir."

"That's well. And, sir," he continued, suddenly stopping short, and turning full on Varbarriere—"for God's sake, *do* you think it is *certainly true?*"

"You had better come, sir, and judge for yourself," pursued Varbarriere.

"D—— you, sir—you think I'll wait over your cursed riddles. I'd as soon wait in hell, sir. You don't know, sir—it's the tortures of the damned. Egad, no man has a right—no man could stand it."

"I think it *is*, sir. I think it's *true*, sir. I *think* it's true. I'm nearly *sure* it's true," answered Varbarriere, with a pallid frown, not minding his anathema. "How *can* I say more?"

General Lennox looked for a while on the ground, then up and about dismally, and gave his neck a little military shake, as if his collar sat uneasily.

"A lonely life for me, sir. I wish to God the villain had shot me first. I was very fond of her, sir—desperately fond—madness, sir. I was thinking I would go back to India. Maybe you'll advise with me, sir, to-morrow? I have no one."

CHAPTER XXI.

At the Green Chamber.

As they approached the house, Jacques, who sat awaiting M. Varbarriere's return, behind the door facing the conservatory, was disagreeably surprised by a visit from the butler.

"Here I am!" exclaimed Jacques very cheerfully, feeling that he could not escape.

"Ow! haw! Mr. Jack, by gad!" exclaimed the butler, actually jumping back in panic, and nearly extinguishing his candle on his breast.

It was his custom, on hearing a noise or seeing a light, to make a ceremonious reconnoissance in assertion of his character, not of course in expectation of finding anything; and here at length he thought he had lighted on a burglar, and from the crown of his head to his heels froze thrills of terror. "And what the devil, Mr. Jack, are you doing here, please, sir?"

"Waiting, my friend, to admit Monsieur, my master," answered Jacques, who was adroit enough to know that it is sometimes cunning to be frank.

In fact it was the apparition of M. Varbarriere, in his queer hat and cloak, crossing a window, which had inspired the butler with a resolution to make his search.

"Haw! dear me! yes, I saw him, Mr. Jack, I did; and what, Mr. Jack, is the doors opened for at these hours, unbeknown to me?"

"My most dear friend, I am taking every care, as you see; but my master, he choose to go out, and he choose to come in. Jacques is nothing but what you call the latch-key."

"And what is he a-doing hout o' doors this time o' night, Mr. Jack? I never knowd afore sich a think to 'appen. Why it looks like a stragethim, that's what it does, Mr. Jack—a stragethim."

And the butler nodded with the air of a moral constable.

"It's a folly, Monsieur. My faith! a little *ruse* of love, I imagine."

"You don't mean to say he's hout a-larkin?"

Jacques, who only conjectured the sense of the sentence, winked and smiled.

"Well, I don't think it's not the way he should be."

"My master is most generous man. My friend, you shall see he shall know how kind you have been. Monsieur, my master, he is a *prince*!" murmured Jacques, eloquently, his fingers on the butler's cuff, and drew back to read in his countenance how it worked.

"It must not hoccur again, Mr. Jack, wile ere," replied the butler, with another grave shake of his head.

"Depend yourself on me," whispered Jacques again in his ear, while he squeezed the prudent hand of the butler affectionately. "But you must go way."

"I do depend on you, Mr. Jack, but I don't like it, mind—I don't like it, and I won't say nothink of it till I hear more from you."

So the butler withdrew, and the danger disappeared.

"You will please to remember, sir," said Varbarriere, as they approached the house, "that this is of the nature of a military movement—a surprise; there must be no sound—no alarm."

"Quite so," whispered old Lennox, with white lips. He was clutching something nervously under the wide sleeve of his loose drab overcoat. He stopped under the shadow of a noble clump of trees about fifty steps away from the glass door they were approaching.

"I—I almost wish, sir—I'll go back—I don't think I can go on, sir."

Varbarriere looked at his companion with an unconscious sneer, but said nothing.

"By ——, sir, if I find it true, I'll kill him, sir."

The old man had in his gouty grip one of those foolish daggers once so much in vogue, but which have now gone out of use, and Varbarriere saw it glimmer in the faint light.

"Surely, Colonel Lennox, you don't mean—you can't mean—you're not going to resort to violence, sir?"

"By ——, sir, he had best look to it."

Varbarriere placed his hand on the old man's sleeve, he could feel the tremor of his thin wrist through it.

"General Lennox, if I had fancied that you could have harboured such a thought, I never should have brought you here."

The General, with his teeth clenched, made him no reply but a fierce nod.

"Remember, sir, you have the courts of law, and you have the code of honour—either or both. One step more I shall not take with you, if you mean that sort of violence."

"What do you mean, sir?" asked the General, grimly.

"I mean this, sir, you shall learn nothing by this night's procedure, unless you promise me, upon your honour as a soldier, sir, and a gentleman, that you will not use that dagger or any other weapon."

General Lennox looked at him with a rather glassy stare.

"You're right, sir, I dare say," said Lennox, suddenly and helplessly.

"You promise?"

"Ay, sir."

"Upon your honour?"

"Upon my honour; ay, sir, my honour."

"I'm satisfied, General. Now observe, you must be silent, and as noiseless as you can. If Sir Jekyl be apprised of your arrival, of course the—the experiment fails."

General Lennox nodded. Emerging into the moonlight, Varbarriere saw how pale and lean his face looked.

Across the grass they pace side by side in silence. The glass door opened without a creak or a hitch. Jacques politely secured it, and, obeying his master's gesture, led the way through the gallery to the hall.

"You'll remember, General, that you arrived late; you understand? and having been observed by me, were admitted; and—and all the rest occurred naturally."

"Yes, sir, any d—d lie you like. All the world's lying—why should not I?"

At the foot of the staircase Jacques was dismissed, having lighted bed-room candles for the two gentlemen, so that they lost something of their air of Spanish conspirators, and they mounted the stairs together in a natural and domestic fashion.

When they had crossed the lobby, and stood at the door of the dressing-room, Varbarriere laid his hand on General Lennox's arm—

"Stop here a moment; you must knock at Lady Alice's door over there, and get the key of your room. She locks the door and keeps the key at night. Make no noise, you know."

They had been fortunate hitherto in having escaped observation; and Varbarriere's strategy had, up to this point, quite succeeded.

"Very quietly, mind," whispered he, and withdrew behind the angle of the wall, toward the staircase.

Old Lennox was by this time at the door which he had indicated, and knocked. There was a little fuss audible within, but no answer. He knocked again more sharply, and he heard the gabble of female voices; and at last a rather nervous inquiry, "Who's there, please?"

"General Lennox, who wants the key of his room," answered he, in no mood to be trifled with. The General was standing, grim as fate, and stark as Corporal Trim, bed-room candle in hand, outside her door.

"He's *not* General Lennox—send him about his business," exclaimed an imperious female voice from the state bed, in which Lady Alice was sitting, measuring some mysterious drops in a graduated glass.

"My lady says she's sorry she can't find it to-night, sir, being at present in bed, please, sir."

"Come, child—no nonsense—I want my key, and I'll have it," replied the General, so awfully that the maid recoiled.

"I think, my lady, he'll be rude if he doesn't get it."

"What's the man like?"

"A nice-spoken gentleman, my lady, and dressed very respectable."

"You never *saw* General Lennox?"

"No, my lady, please."

Neither had Lady Alice; but she had heard him minutely described.

"A lean ugly old man is he, with white bristly whiskers, you know, and a white head, and little grey eyes, eh?"

They had no notion that their little confidence was so distinctly audible to the General without, who stood eyeing the panel fiercely as a sentry would a suspicious figure near his beat, and with fingers twitching with impatience to clutch his key.

"What sort of nose?" demanded the unseen speaker—"long or short?"

"Neither, please, my lady; bluish, rayther, I should say."

"But it is either long or short, *decidedly*, and I forget which," said Lady Alice—"'*Tis*n't he!"

The General ground his teeth with impatience, and knocked so sharp a signal at the door that Lady Alice bounced in her bed.

"Lord bless us! How dare he do that?—tell him how dare he."

"Lady Alice, sir, would be much obliged if you'd be so good not knock so loud, sir, please," said the maid at the door, translating the message.

"Tell your mistress I'm General Lennox, and must have my key," glared the General, and the lady's-maid, who was growing nervous, returned.

"He looks, my lady, like he'd beat us, please, if he does not get the key, my lady."

"Sha'n't have it, the brute! We don't know he is—a robber, maybe. Bolt the door, and tell him to bring Monsieur Varbarriere to the lobby, and if *he* says he's General Lennox he shall have the key."

With trembling fingers the maid *did* bolt the door, and once more accost the soldier, who was chafing on the threshold.

"Please, sir, my lady is not well, having nervous pains, please sir, in her head to-night, and therefore would be 'appy if you would be so kind to bring Mister Barvarrian" (the name by which our corpulent friend was known in the servants' hall) "to her door, please, when she'll try what she may do to oblige you, sir."

"They don't know me," said the General, accosting Varbarriere, who was only half a dozen steps removed, and whom he had rejoined. "You must come to the door, they say, and tell them it's all right."

Perhaps with some inward sense of the comic, Varbarriere presented himself at the door, when, his voice being recognised, and he himself reconnoitred through the keyhole and reported upon, the maid presented herself in an extemporised drapery of cloaks and shawls, like a traveller in winter, and holding these garments together with one hand, with the other presented the key, peering anxiously in the General's face.

"Key, sir, please."

"I thank you," said the General, with a nod, to which she responded with such a courtesy as her costume permitted. The door shut, and as the gentlemen withdrew they heard the voices of the inmates again busy with the subject.

"Good-night," whispered Varbarriere, looking in the General's blue eye with his own full and steady gaze.

"I know you'll remember your promise," said he.

"Yes—what?"

"No *violence*" replied Varbarriere.

"No, of course, I said so. Good-bye."

"You must appear—your *manner*, mind—just as usual. Nothing to alarm—you may defeat all else."

"I see."

Varbarriere pressed his hand encouragingly. It felt like death.

"Don't fear me," said General Lennox. "We'll see—we'll see, sir; good-bye."

He spoke in a low, short, resolute tone, almost defiant; but looked very ill. Varbarriere had never taken leave of a man on the drop, but thought that this must be like it.

He beckoned to him as the General moved toward the dressing-room door, and made an earnest signal of silence. Lennox nodded, applied the key, and Varbarriere was gone.

CHAPTER XXII.

In the Green Chamber.

General Lennox opened the door suddenly, and stood in the green chamber, holding his candle above his temple, and staring with a rather wild countenance and a gathered brow to the further end of the room. A candle burned on the table, and the Bible lay beside it. No one was there but the inmate of the bed, who sat up with a scared face. He locked the door in silence, and put the key in his pocket.

"Who's there?—who is it? O my God! Arthur, is it you?" she cried. It was not a welcome. It was as if she had seen a ghost—but she smiled.

"You're well? quite well? and happy? no doubt happy?" said Lennox, setting down his candle on the table near the bed, "and glad to see me?"

"Yes, Arthur; Arthur, what's the matter? You're ill—*are* you ill?"

"Ho! no, very well, quite well—very well indeed."

There was that in his look and manner that told her she was ruined. She froze with a horror she had never dreamed of before.

"There's something, Arthur—there is—you won't tell me."

"That's strange, and *you* tell *me* everything."

"What do you *mean*, sir? Oh, Arthur, what *do* you mean?"

"Mean! Nothing!"

"I was afraid you were angry, and I've done nothing to vex you—nothing. You looked so angry—it's so unreasonable and odd of you. But I am glad to see you, though you don't seem glad to see me. You've been a long time away, Arthur, in London, very long. I hope all your business is settled, I hope. And I'm very glad to hear you're not ill—indeed I am. Why are you vexed?"

"Vexed! ho! I'm vexed, am I? that's odd."

She was making a desperate effort to seem as usual, and talked on.

"We have had old Lady Alice Redcliffe here, my chaperon, all this while, if you please, and takes such ridiculous care of me, and locks me into my room every night. She means kindly, but it is very foolish."

"Yes, it is, d—d foolish."

"We have been employed very much as usual—walking, and driving, and croquet. Beatrix and I have been very much together, and Sir Paul and Lady Blunket still here. I don't think we have had any arrival since you left us. Mr. Guy Strangways has gone away, and Monsieur Varbarriere returned to-day."

She was gabbling as merrily as she could, feeling all the time on the point of fainting.

"And the diamonds came?" the General said, suddenly, with a sort of laugh.

"Oh! yes, the diamonds, so beautiful. I did not thank you in my letter—not half enough. They are beautiful—so exquisitely beautiful—brilliants—and so becoming; you have no idea. I hope you got my letter. Indeed I felt it all, every word, Arthur, only I could not say half what I wished. Don't you believe me, Arthur?"

"Lie down, woman, and take your sleep; you sleep *well*? you *all* do—of course you sleep? Lie down."

"You are angry, Arthur; you are excited; something has happened—something bad—what is it? For God's sake, Arthur, tell me what it is. Why won't you tell me?"

"Nothing—nothing strange—quite common."

"Oh! Arthur, tell me at once, or kill me. You look as if you hated me."

"*Hate* you!—There's a hereafter. God sees."

"I can't understand you, Arthur; you wish to distract me. I'd rather know anything. For mercy's sake speak out."

"Lie you down, and wait."

She did lie down. The hour of judgment had come as a thief in the night. The blood in her temples seemed to drum on the pillow. There was not a clear thought in her brain, only the one stunning consciousness.

"He knows all! I am ruined." Yet the feminine instinct of *finesse* was not quite overpowered.

Having placed the candle on the chimneypiece, so that the curtain at the foot of the bed throw its shadow over that recess in which the sorcerer Varbarriere had almost promised to show the apparition, old Lennox sat down at the bedside, next this mysterious point of observation. Suddenly it crossed him, as a break of moonlight will the blackest night of storm, that he must act more wisely. Had he not alarmed his wife?—what signal might not be contrived to warn off her guilty accomplice?

"Jennie," said he, with an effort, in a more natural tone, "I'm tired, very tired. We'll sleep. I'll tell you all in the morning. Go to sleep."

"Good-night," she murmured.

"That will do; go to sleep," he answered.

Gently, gently, she stole a peep at that pretty watch that stood in its little slanting stand at her bedside. There was still twenty minutes— Heaven be praised for its mercy!—and she heard old Lennox at the far side of this "great bed of Ware," making an ostentation of undressing. His boots tumbled on the floor. She heard his watchguard jingle on the stand, and his keys and purse dropped in turn on the table. She heard him adjust the chair, as usual, on which he was wont to deposit his clothes as he removed them; she fancied she even heard him yawn. Her heart was throbbing as though it would choke her, and she was praying as she never prayed before— for a reprieve. And yet her respiration was long and deep, as if in the sleep she was counterfeiting.

Lennox, at the other side, put off his muffler, his outer coat, the frock-coat he wore, the waistcoat. She dared not look round to observe his progress. But at last he threw himself on the bed with a groan of fatigue, and pulled the coverlet over him, and lay without motion, like a man in need of rest.

Lady Jane listened. She could not hear him breathe. She waited some five minutes, and then she murmured, "Arthur." No answer. "*Arthur.*" Again no answer; and she raised herself on her elbow, cautiously, and listened; and after a little pause, quick as light she got out of bed, glided to the chimneypiece, and lighted a taper at the candle there, listened again for a moment, and on tiptoe, in bare feet, glided round the foot of the bed, and approached the recess at the other side of the bed's head, and instantly her fingers were on one of those little flowers in the ormolu arabesque that runs along the edge of the wooden casing.

Before she could turn it a gouty hand over her shoulder took hold of hers, and, with a low sudden cry, she saw her husband.

"Can't I do that for you? What is it?" said he.

Her lips were white, and she gazed in his face without saying a word.

He was standing there unbooted, in his trowsers, with those crimson silk suspenders on, with the embroidery of forget-me-nots, which she had described as "her work"—I am afraid inaccurately—a love-token—hypocrisy on hypocrisy.

Asmodeus, seated on the bed's head, smirked down sardonically on the tableau, and clapped his apish hands.

"Get to your bed there. If you make a sign, by ——, I'll kill you."

She made no answer. She gazed at him dumbly. He was not like himself. He looked like a villain.

He did not lie down again. He sat by the little table, on which his watch, his keys, and loose shillings lay. The night was chill, but he did not feel it then.

He sat in his shirt-sleeves, his chin on his breast, eyeing from under his stern white brows the shadowy arch through which the figure was to emerge.

Suddenly he heard the swift steps of little, naked feet on the carpet come round the foot of the bed, and his wife wildly threw herself at his feet, and clasped them in an agony. He could feel every sinew in her arms vibrate in the hysterical strain of her entreaty.

"Oh, Arthur! oh, darling, take me away from this, for God's sake. Come down with me; come to the drawing-room, or to the dressing-room; take me away; you'll be happier, indeed you will, than ever you were; you'll never repent it, darling; do what I say. I'll be the best wife, indeed I will. See, I've been reading my Bible; look at it. I'm quite changed—quite changed. God only knows how changed. Oh, Arthur, Arthur, if you ever loved me, take me away; come from this room—come, you'll never repent it. Oh, Arthur, be wise, be merciful! The more you forgive the more you'll be loved. It is not I, but God says that. I'm praying to you as I would to Him, and He forgives us when we implore: take pity on me; you'll never be sorry. Have mercy, Arthur, have mercy—you are kind, I know you're kind, you would not ruin your wretched Jennie. Oh, take pity before it is too late, and take me from this dreadful room. You'll be glad, indeed you will; there never was such a wife as I'll be to you, the humblest, the most loving, and you'll be happier than ever you were. Oh, Arthur, Arthur, I'm praying to you as if you were God, for mercy; don't say no! Oh, can you; can you; can you?"

General Lennox was moved, but not from his course. He never saw before such a face of misery. It was like the despairing pleading of the last day. But alas! in this sort of quarrel there can be no compromise; reconciliation is dishonour.

"Go and lie down. It's all over between us," said he in a tone that left her no room for hope. With a low, long cry, and her fingers clasped over her forehead, she retraced her steps, and lay down, and quietly drew her icy feet into the bed, awaiting the inevitable. Lennox resumed his watch.

CHAPTER XXIII.

The Morning.

Monsieur Varbarriere was standing all this while with his shadow to the door-post of the Window dressing-room, and his dark eyes fixed on the further door which admits to the green chamber. His bedroom candle, which was dwindling, stood on the table at his elbow.

He heard a step crossing the lobby softly toward his own room, and whispered,

"Who's there?"

"Jacques Duval, at Monsieur's service."

Monsieur took his candle, and crossed the floor to meet Jacques, who was approaching, and he signed to him to stop. He looked at his watch. It was now twenty minutes past one.

"Jacques," said he, in a whisper, "there's no mistake about those sounds?"

"No, Monsieur, not at all."

"Three nights running, you say?"

"Monsieur is perfectly right."

"Steps, you say?"

"Yes, sir, footsteps."

"It could not have been the wind, the shaking or creaking of the floor or windows?"

"Ah no, Monsieur, not at all as that."

"The steps quick, not slow; wasn't it?"

"Quick, sir, as one in haste and treading lightly would walk."

"And this as you sat in the butler's room?"

"Monsieur recollects exactly."

Varbarriere knew that the butler's room exactly underlay that dingy library that abutted on Sir Jekyl's bedchamber, and on that account had placed his sentinel to watch there.

"Always about the same time?" he asked.

"Very nearly, Monsieur, a few minutes, sometimes before, sometimes after; only trifle, in effect *nothing*," answered Jacques.

"Jacques, you must leave my door open, so that, should I want you, you can hear me call from the door of that dressing-room; take care you keep awake, but don't move."

So saying, Varbarriere returned to his place of observation. He set down his candle near the outer door, and listened, glowering as before at the far one. The crisis was near at hand, so near that, on looking at his watch again, he softly approached the door of the green chamber, and there, I am sorry to say, he listened diligently.

But all was disappointingly silent for a while longer. Suddenly he heard a noise. A piece of furniture shoved aside it seemed, a heavy step or two, and the old man's voice exclaim "Ha!" with an interrogatory snarl in it. There was a little laugh, followed by a muffled blow or a fall, and a woman's cry, sharp and momentary— "Oh, God! oh, God!" and a gush of smothered sobs, and the General's grim voice calling "silence!" and a few stern words from him, and fast talking between them, and Lady Jane calling for light, and then more wild sobbing. There had been no sound of a struggle.

Varbarriere stood, stooping, scowling, open-mouthed, at the door, with his fingers on the handle, hardly breathing. At last he gasped—

"That d—— old ape! has he hurt her?" He listened, but all was silent. Did he still hear smothered sobs? He could not be certain. His eyes were glaring on the panel of the door; but on his retina was a ghostly image of beautiful Lady Jane, blood-stained, with glazing eyes, like Cleopatra dying of her asps.

After a while he heard some words from the General in an odd ironical tone. Then came silence again—continued silence—half an hour's silence, and then a sound of some one stirring.

He knew the tread of the General about the room. Whatever was to occur *had* occurred. That was his conclusion. Perhaps the General was coming to *his* room to look for him. It was time he should withdraw, and so he did.

"You may get to your bed, Jacques, and come at the usual hour."

So, with his accustomed civilities, Monsieur Jacques disappeared. But old Lennox did not visit Varbarriere, nor even emerge from his room.

After an hour Varbarriere revisited the dressing-room next the green chamber. He waited long without hearing anything, and at length he heard a step—was it the General's again, or Sir Jekyl's?—whoever it was, he seemed to be fidgeting about the room, collecting and packing his things, Varbarriere fancied, for a journey; and then he heard him draw the writing-table a little, and place a chair near it, and as the candle was shining through the keyhole, he supposed the General had placed himself to write at it.

Something had happened, he felt sure. Had Lennox despatched Sir Jekyl, or Sir Jekyl wounded the General? Or had Lady Jane been killed? Or was all right, and no one of the actors stretched on the green baize carpet before the floats? He would believe that, and got quickly to his bed, nursing that comfortable conclusion the while. But when he shut his eyes, a succession of pale faces smeared with blood came and looked at him, and would not be ordered away. So he lighted his candle again, and tried to exorcise these visitors with the pages of a French Review, until very late sleep overtook him.

Jacques was in his room at the usual hour, eight o'clock; and Varbarriere started up in his bed at the sound of his voice, with a confused anticipation of a catastrophe. But the cheerful squire had nothing to relate except how charming was the morning, and to hand a letter to Monsieur.

Varbarriere's mind was not upon letters that morning, but on matters nearer home.

"General Lennox has not been down-stairs yet?"

"No, Monsieur."

"Nor Sir Jekyl?"

"No, Monsieur."

"Where's my watch? there—yes—eight o'clock. H'm. When does Lady Jane's maid go to her?"

"Not until the General has advanced himself pretty well in his toilet, the entrance being through his dressing-room."

"The General used to be down early?"

"Yes, Monsieur, half-past eight I remember."

"And Sir Jekyl?"

"About the same hour."

"And Lady Jane is called, I suppose, a little before that hour?"

"Yes, about a quarter past eight, Monsieur. Will Monsieur please to dcsirc his cup of coffee?"

"Yes, everything—quickly—I wish to dress; and what's this? a letter."

It was from Guy Deverell, as Varbarriere saw at a glance, and not through the post.

"My nephew hasn't come?" sternly demanded Varbarriere, with a kind of start, on reading the signature, which he did before reading the letter.

"No, Monsieur, a young man has conveyed it from Slowton."

Whereupon Varbarriere, with a striped silk nightcap of many colours pending over his corrugated forehead, read the letter through the divided bed-curtains.

His nephew, it appeared, had arrested his course at Birmingham, and turned about, and reached Slowton again about the hour at which M. Varbarriere had met old Lennox in the grounds of Marlowe.

"What a fanfaronnade! These young fellows—what asses they are!" sneered Varbarriere.

It was not, in truth, very wise. This handsome youth announced his intention to visit Marlowe that day, to see Monsieur Varbarriere for, perhaps, the last time before setting forth for Algeria, where he knew a place would at once be found for him in the ranks of those brave soldiers whom France had sent there. His gratitude to his uncle years could never abate, but it was time he should cease to task his generosity, and he was quite resolved henceforward to fight his way single-handed in the world, as so many other young fellows did. Before taking his departure he thought he should present himself to say his adieux to M. Varbarriere—even to his host, Sir Jekyl Marlowe; and there was a good deal more of such stuff.

"Sir Jekyl! stuff! His uncle! lanterns! He wants to see that pretty Miss Beatrix once more! *voila tout!* He has chosen his time well. Who knows what confusion may be here to day? No matter."

By this time he had got his great quilted dressing-gown about him, in the folds of which Varbarriere looked more unwieldy still than in his drawing-room costume.

"I must read about that Algeria; have they got any diseases there? plague—yellow fever—ague! By my faith! if the place is tolerably healthy, it would be no such bad plan to let the young fool take a turn on that gridiron, and learn thoroughly the meaning of independence."

So Monsieur Varbarriere, with a variety of subjects to think over, pursued his toilet.

CHAPTER XXIV.

The Doctor's Visit.

Sir Jekyl's hour was eight o'clock, and punctually his man, Tomlinson, knocked at his door.

"Hollo! Is that Tomlinson?" answered the voice from within.

"Yes, sir, please."

"See, Tomlinson, I say, it's very ridiculous; but I'm hanged if I can stir, that confounded gout's got hold of my foot again. You'll have to force the door. Send some one down to the town for Doctor Pratt—d'ye see?—and get me some handkerchiefs, and don't be all day."

The faithful Tomlinson listening, with a snowy shirt and a pair of socks on his arm and the tips of his fingers fiddling with the door-handle, listening at the other side of the panel, with forehead inclined forward and mouth open, looked, I am sorry to say, a good deal amused, although he answered in a concerned tone; and departed to execute his orders.

"Guv'nor took in toe again," he murmured, with a solemn leer, as he paused before the butler's broad Marseilles waistcoat.

"As how?" inquired he.

"The gout; can't stir a peg, and he's locked hisself in, as usual, over night."

"Lawk!" exclaimed the butler, and I dare say both would have liked to laugh, but neither cared to compromise himself.

"Chisel and mallet, Mr. Story, we shall want, if you please, and some one to go at once for the doctor to the town."

"I know—yes—hinstantly," ejaculated the butler.

So things proceeded. Pratt, M. D., the medical practitioner of the village, whose yellow hall door and broad brass plate, and shop window round the corner, with the two time-honoured glass jars, one of red the other of green fluid, representing physic in its most attractive hues, were not more widely known than his short, solemn, red face, blue chin, white whiskers, and bald pate, was roused by the messenger's summons, at his toilet, and peeped over his muslin blind to discover the hand that was ringing so furiously among his withered hollyhocks; and at the same time Tomlinson and the butler were working with ripping chisel, mallet, and even a poker, to effect an entrance.

"Ha! Dives," said the Baronet, as that divine, who had heard the sad news, presented himself at the now open door. "I sent for you, my dear fellow. A horrid screw in my left toe this time. Such a spoil-sport! curse it, but it won't be anything. I've sent for Pratt, and you'll tell the people at breakfast, you know, that I'm a prisoner; only a trifle though, I hope—down to dinner maybe. There's the gong—run down, like a dear fellow."

"Not flying—well fixed in the toe, eh?" said Dives, rather anxiously, for he did not like Sir Jekyl's constrained voice and sunken look.

"Quite fixed—blazing away—just the thing Pratt likes—confounded pain though. Now run down, my dear fellow, and make my excuses, but say I hope to be down to dinner, mind."

So, with another look, Dives went down, not quite comfortable, for on the whole he liked Jekyl, who had done a great deal for him; he did not like tragedies, he was very comfortable as he stood, and quite content to await the course of nature.

"Is that d—d doctor *ever* coming?" asked Sir Jekyl, dismally.

"He'll be here, sir, please, in five minutes—so he said, sir."

"I know, but there's been *ten* since, curse him."

"Shall I send again, sir?" asked Tomlinson.

"Do; say I'm in pain, and can't think what the devil's keeping him."

Beatrix in a moment more came running up in consternation.

"How do you feel now, papa? Gout, is it not?" she asked, having obtained leave to come in; "not very bad, I hope."

The Baronet smiled with an effort.

"Gout's never very pleasant, a hot thumb-screw on one's toe, my dear, but that's all; it will be nothing. Pratt's coming, and he'll get me right in a day or two—only the great toe. I beg pardon for naming it so often—very waspish though, that's all. Don't stay away, or the people will fancy something serious; and possibly I may be down, in a slipper though, to dinner. So run down, Trixie, darling."

And Trixie, with the same lingering look that Dives had cast on him, only more anxious, betook herself to the parlour as he had desired.

In a little while Doctor Pratt had arrived. As he toddled through the hall he encountered the Rev. Dives on his way to the breakfast-parlour. Pratt had suffered some rough handling and damage at the hands of Time, and Dives was nothing the better of the sarcastic manipulations of the same ancient god, since they had last met. Still they instantly recognised, and shook hands cordially, and when the salutation was over—

"Well, and what's wrong with the Baronet?"

"Gout; he drinks two glasses of port, I've observed, at dinner, and it always disagrees with him. Pray do stop it—the port, I mean."

"Hand or foot?"

"The great toe—the best place, isn't it?"

"No better, sir. There's nothing, nothing of the stomach?—I brought this in *case*," and he held up a phial.

"No, but I don't like his looks; he looks so haggard and exhausted."

"H'm, I'd like to see him at once; I don't know his room though."

So Dives put him in charge of a guide, and they parted.

"Well, Sir Jekyl, how d'ye do, hey? and how's all this? Old enemy, hey—all in the foot—fast in the toe—isn't he?" began the Doctor as he entered the Baronet's room.

"Ay, in the toe. Sit down there, Pratt, beside me."

"Ah, ha! nervous; you think I'll knock him, eh? Ha, ha, ha! No, no, no! Don't be afraid. Nothing wrong in the stomach—no chill—retching?"

"No."

"*Head* all right, too; nothing queer there?"

"Nothing."

"Nothing in the knuckles—old acquaintance, you know, when you meet, sometimes a squeeze by the hand, eh? Ha, ha, ha!"

"No, nothing in the hand," said the Baronet, a little testily.

"Nor any wandering sensations here, you know, and there, hey?" said the little fellow, sitting down briskly by his patient.

"No; curse it."

"Troublesome to talk, hey?" asked Pratt, observing that he seemed faint, and talked low and with effort.

"No—yes—that is, *tired*."

"I see, no pain; all nicely fixed in the toe; *that* could not be better, and what do you refer it to? By Jove, it's eighteen, *nineteen* months since your last! When you came down to Dartbroke, for the Easter, you know, and wrote to me for the thing with the ether, hey? You've been at that d—d bin, I'm afraid, the forbidden fruit, hey? Egad, sir, I call it fluid gout, and the crust nothing but chalk-stone."

"*No—I haven't,*" croaked the Baronet savagely.

"Ha, ha, ha!" laughed the Doctor, drumming on his fat knee with his stethoscope. "Won't admit—won't allow, hey?" As he spoke he was attempting to take him by the wrist.

"Pulse? How are we there, eh?"

"Turn that d—d fellow out of the room, and bolt the door, will you?" muttered Sir Jekyl, impatiently.

"Hey? I see. How are *you*, Mr. Tomlinson—no return of that bronchial annoyance, eh? I'll ask you just now—we'll just make Sir Jekyl Marlowe a little more comfortable first, and I've a question or two—we'd be as well alone, you see—and do you mind? You'll be in the way, you know; we may want you, you know."

So the docile Tomlinson withdrew with a noiseless alacrity, and Doctor Pratt, in deference to his patron, bolted the mangled door.

"See, Pratt, you're tiring me to death, with your beastly questions. Wait, will you? Sit down. You'll promise me you won't tell this to anyone."

"What?"

"Do hold your tongue, like a dear fellow, and listen. Upon your honour, you don't tell, till I give you leave, what's the matter with me. Come—d—— you; yes or no?"

"Well, you know I must, if you insist; but I'd rayther not."

"You *must*. On your honour you won't tell, and you'll call it gout?"

"Why—why, if it *is* not gout, eh? don't you see? it would not *do*."

"Well, good morning to you, Doctor Pratt, for I'm hanged if you prescribe for me on any other terms."

"Well, don't you see, I say I must, if you insist, don't you see; it may be—it may be—egad! it might be very serious to let you wait."

"You promise?"

"Yes, I *do. There!*"

"Gout, mind, and nothing else; all gout, upon your honour."

"Aw, well! *Yes.*"

"Upon your *honour*; why the devil can't you speak!"

"Upon my honour, of course."

"You kill me, making me talk. Well, 'tisn't in the toe—it's up here," and he uncovered his right shoulder and chest, showing some handkerchiefs and his night-shirt soaked in blood.

"What the devil's all this?" exclaimed the Doctor, rising suddenly, and the ruddy tints of his face fading into a lilac hue. "Why—why, you're *hurt*; egad, you're hurt. We must examine it. What is it with—how the plague did it all come about?"

"The act of God," answered Sir Jekyl, with a faint irony in his tone.

"The—ah!—well, I don't understand."

"I mean the purest accident."

"Bled a lot, egad! These things seem pretty dry—bleeding away *still*? You must not keep it so hot—the sheet only."

"I think it's stopped—the things are sticking—I feel them."

"So much the better; but we must not leave it this way—and—and I daren't disturb it, you know, without help, so we'll have to take Tomlinson into confidence."

"'Gad, you'll do no such thing."

"But, my dear sir, I *must* tell you, this thing, whatever it is, looks very serious. I can *tell* you, it's not to be trifled with, and this sort of nonsense may be as much as your life's worth, egad."

"You shan't," said Sir Jekyl.

"You'll allow me to speak with your brother?"

"No, you shan't."

"Ho, now, Sir Jekyl, really now—"

"Promised—your honour."

"'Tisn't a fair position," said the practitioner, shaking his head, with his hands stuffed in his pockets, and staring dismally at the blood-stained linen. "I'll tell you what we must do—there are two supernumeraries I happen to know at the county hospital, and Hicks is a capital nurse. I'll write a line and they'll send her here. There's a room in there, eh? yes, well, she can be quartered *there*, and talk with no one but you and me; in fact, see no one except in your presence, don't you see? and egad, we *must* have her, or I'll give up the *case*."

"Well, yes; send for her."

CHAPTER XXV.

The Patient interrogated.

So Doctor Pratt scribbled a few lines on the back of his card, and Tomlinson was summoned to the door, and told to expedite its despatch, and "send one of the men in a dog-cart as hard as he could peg, and to be sure to see Doctor Hoggins," who had been an apprentice once of honest Pratt's.

"Tell her not to wait for dressing, or packing, or anything. She'll come just as she is, and we'll send again for her things, d'ye mind? and let him drive quick. It's only two miles, he must not be half an hour about it;" and in a low whisper, with a frown and a nod, he added to Tomlinson on the lobby, "I *want* her here."

So he sat down very grave by Sir Jekyl, and took his pulse, very low and inflammatory, he thought.

"You lost a good deal of blood? It is not all here, eh?"

"No; I lost some beside."

"Mind, now, don't move. You may bring it on again; and you're not in a condition to spare any. How did it happen?"

"A knife or something."

"A thrust, eh? Not a *cut*; I mean a *stab*?"

"Yes."

"About how long ago? What hour?"

Sir Jekyl hesitated.

"Oh! now come, Sir Jekyl, I beg pardon, but I really must know the *facts*."

"Remember your promise—awfully tired."

"Certainly. What o'clock?"

"Between one and two."

"You must have some claret;" and he opened the door and issued orders accordingly. The Doctor had his fingers on his pulse by this time.

"Give me some water; I'm dying of thirst," said the patient.

The Doctor obeyed.

"And there's no gout at all, then?" said he.

"Not a bit," answered Sir Jekyl, pettishly; his temper and his breath seemed to be failing him a little.

"Did you feel faint when it happened, or after?"

"Just for a moment, when it happened, then pretty well; and when I got here, in a little time, worse, very faint; I think I did faint, but a little blood always does that for me. But it's not deep, I know by the feel—only the muscle."

"H'm. I shan't disturb these things till the nurse comes; glad there's no gout, no complication."

The claret-jug was soon at the bedside, and the Doctor helped his patient to a few spoonfuls, and felt his pulse again.

"I must go home for the things, d'ye see? I shan't be long away though. Here, Tomlinson, you'll give Sir Jekyl a spoonful or a glassful of this claret, d'ye mind, as often as he requires it. About every ten minutes a little to wet his lips; and mind, now, Sir Jekyl, drink any quantity rather than let yourself go down."

As he went from the room he signed to Tomlinson, who followed him quietly.

"See, now, my good fellow, this is rather a serious case, you understand me; and he must not be let down. Your master, Sir Jekyl,

I say, he must be kept up. Keep a little claret to his lips, and if you see any pallor or moisture in his face, give it him by a glassful at a time; and go on, do you mind, till he begins to look natural again, for he's in a very critical state; and if he were to faint, d'ye see, or anything, it might be a very serious thing; and you'd better ring for another bottle or two; but don't leave him on any account."

They were interrupted here by a tapping in Sir Jekyl's room. Lying on his back, he was rapping with his penknife on the table.

"Why the plague don't you come?" he muttered, as Tomlinson drew near. "Where's Pratt? tell him I want him."

"Hey—no—no *pain*?" asked the Doctor.

"No; I want to know—I want to know what the devil you've been saying to him out there."

"Nothing; only a direction."

"Do you think—do you think I'm in *danger*?" said Sir Jekyl.

"Well, *no*. You needn't be if you mind, but—but don't refuse the claret, mind, and don't be afraid of it if you feel a—a sinking, you know, any quantity; and I'll be back before the nurse comes from the hospital; and—and don't be excited, for you'll do very well if you'll only do as I tell you."

The Doctor nodded, standing by the bed, but he did not look so cheerfully as he spoke.

"I'll be back in twenty minutes. Don't be fidgety, you know; don't stir, and you'll do very nicely, I say."

When the Doctor was gone, Sir Jekyl said—

"Tomlinson."

"Yes, sir, please."

"Tomlinson, come here; let me see you."

"Yes, Sir Jekyl; sir—"

"I say, Tomlinson, you'll tell the truth, mind."

"Yes, sir, please."

"Did that fellow say anything?"

"Yes, sir, please."

"Out with it."

"'Twas claret, Sir Jekyl, please, sir."

"None of your d—d lies, sir. I heard him say 'serious.' What *was* it?"

"Please, sir, he said as how you were to be kep up, sir, which it might be serious if otherwise. So he said, sir, please, it might be serious if you was not properly kep up with claret, please, sir."

"Come, Tomlinson—see I *must* know. Did he say I was in a bad way—likely to die?—come." His face was certainly hollow and earthy enough just then to warrant forebodings.

"No, sir; certainly not, sir. No, sir, please, nothing of the kind."

The Baronet looked immeasurably more like himself.

"Give me some wine—a glass," said he.

The Doctor, stumping away rapidly to his yellow door, and red and green twin bottles, in the village, was thinking how the deuce this misadventure of Sir Jekyl's had befallen. The Baronet's unlucky character was well known wherever he resided or had property.

"Who the devil did it, I wonder?" conjectured the Doctor. "Two o'clock at night. Some pretty fury with a scissors, maybe. We'll know time enough; these things always come out—always come out, egad! It's a shame for him getting into scrapes at his time of life."

In the breakfast-parlour, very merry was the party then assembled, notwithstanding the absence of some of its muster-roll. Lady Jane Lennox, an irregular breakfaster, stood excused. Old Lady Alice was no more expected than the portrait of Lady Mary in her bed-room. General Lennox had business that morning, and was not particularly inquired after. Sir Jekyl, indeed, was missed—bustling, good-natured, lively—his guests asked after him with more than a conventional solicitude.

"Well, and how is papa now?" inquired Sir Paul, who knew what gout was, and being likely to know it again, felt a real interest in the Baronet's case. "No *acute* pain, I hope?"

"I'm afraid he *is* in pain, more than he admits," answered Beatrix.

"Tomlinson told me it's all in the—the extremity, though that's well. Intelligent fellow, Tomlinson. Mine is generally what they call atonic, not attended with much pain, you know;" and he illustrated his disquisition by tendering his massive mulberry knuckles for the young lady's contemplation, and fondling them with the glazed fingers of the other hand, while his round blue eyes stared, with a slow sort of wonder, in her face, as if he expected a good deal in the way of remark from the young lady to mitigate his astonishment.

Lady Blunket, who was beside her, relieved this embarrassment, and nodding at her ear, said—

"Flannel—*flannel*, chiefly. Sir Paul, there, his medical man, Doctor Duddle, we have great confidence in *him*—relies very much on warmth. My poor father used to take Regent's—Regent's—I forget what—a *bottle*. But Doctor Duddle would not hear of Sir Paul there attempting to put it to his lips. Regent's—*what* is it? I shall forget my own name soon. *Water* is it? At all events he won't hear of it—diet and flannel, that's his method. My poor father, you know, died of gout, quite suddenly, at Brighton. Cucumber, they said."

And Lady Blunket, overcome by the recollection, touched her eyes with her handkerchief.

"Cucumber and salmon, it was, *I* recollect," said Sir Paul, with a new accession of intelligence.

"But he passed away most happily, Miss Marlowe," continued Lady Blunket. "I have some verses of poor mamma's. *She* was *very* religious, you know; they have been very much admired."

"Ay—yes," said Sir Paul, "he was helped *twice*—very im*pru*dent!"

"I was mentioning dear mamma's verses, you remember."

Sir Paul not being quite so well up in this aspect of the case, simply grunted and became silent; and indeed I don't think he had been so loquacious upon any other morning or topic since his arrival at Marlowe.

"They are beautiful," continued Lady Blunket, "and so resigned. I was most anxious, my dear, to place a tablet under the monument, you know, at Maisly; a mural tablet, just like the Tuftons', you know; they are very reasonable, inscribed with dear mamma's verses; but I can't persuade Sir Paul, he's so poor, you know; but certainly, some day or other, I'll do it myself."

The irony about Sir Paul's poverty, though accompanied by a glance from her ladyship's pink eyes, was lost on that excellent man, who was by this time eating some hot broil.

Their judicious conversation was not without an effect commensurate with the rarity of the exertion, for between them they had succeeded in frightening poor Beatrix a good deal.

In other quarters the conversation was proceeding charmingly. Linnett was describing to Miss Blunket the exploits of a terrier of his, among a hundred rats let loose together—a narrative to which she listened with a pretty girlish alternation of terror and interest; while the Rev. Dives Marlowe and old Doocey conversed earnestly on the virtues of colchicum, and exchanged confidences touching their gouty symptoms and affections; and Drayton, assisted by an occasional parenthesis from that prodigious basso, Varbarriere, was haranguing Beatrix and Mrs. Maberly on pictures, music, and the way to give agreeable dinners; and now Beatrix asked old Lady Blunket in what way she would best like to dispose of the day. What to do, where to drive, an inquiry into which the other ladies were drawn, and the debate, assisted by the gentlemen, grew general and animated.

CHAPTER XXVI.

General Lennox appears.

In the midst of this animation the butler whispered in the ear of the Rev. Dives Marlowe, who, with a grave face, but hardly perceived, slid away, and met the Doctor in the hall.

"Aw—*see*—this is a—rather nasty case, I am bound to tell you, Mr. Marlowe; he's in a rather critical state. He'll see you, I dare say, by-and-by, and I hope he'll get on satisfactorily. I hope he'll *do*; but I must tell you, it's a—it's a—serious *case*, sir."

"Nothing since?" asked Dives, a good deal shocked.

"Nothing since, sir," answered the Doctor, with a nod, and his eyebrows raised as he stood ruminating a little, with his fists in his pockets. "But—but—you'll do *this*, sir, if you please—you'll call in some physician, in whom you have confidence, for I'll tell you frankly, it's not a case in which I'd like to be alone."

"It's very sudden, sir; whom do you advise?" said Dives, looking black and pallid.

"Well, you know, it ought to be *soon*. I'd like him at once—you can't send very far. There's Ponder, I would not desire better, if you approve. Send a fellow riding, and don't spare horse-flesh, mind, to Slowton. He'll find Ponder there if he's quick, and let him bring him in a chaise and four, and pay the fellows well, and they'll not be long coming. They'd better be quick, for there's something must be done, and I can't undertake it alone."

Together they walked out to the stable-yard, Dives feeling stunned and odd. The Doctor was reserved, and only waited to see things in train. Almost while Dives pencilled his urgent note on the back of a letter, the groom had saddled one of the hunters and got into his jacket, and was mounted and away.

Dives returned to the house. From the steps he looked with a sinking heart after the man cantering swiftly down the avenue, and saw him in the distance like a dwindling figure in a dream, and somehow it was to him an effort to remember what it was all about. He felt the cold air stirring his dark locks, streaked with silver, and found he had forgot his hat, and so came in.

"You have seen a great deal of art, Monsieur Varbarriere," said Drayton, accosting that gentleman admiringly, in the outer hall, where they were fitting themselves with their "wide-awakes" and "jerries." "It is so pleasant to meet anyone who really understands it and has a feeling for it. You seem to me to lean more to painting than to statuary."

"Painting is the more popular art, because the more literal. The principles of statuary are abstruse. The one, you see, is a repetition— the other a translation. Colour is more than outline, and the painter commands it. The man with the chisel has only outline, and must render nature into white stone, with the *natural* condition of being inspected from every point, and the *unnatural* one, in solid anatomy, of immobility. It is a greater triumph, but a less effect."

Varbarriere was lecturing this morning, according to his lights, more copiously and *ex cathedrâ* than usual. Perhaps his declamations and antithesis represented the constraint which he placed on himself, like those mental exercises which sleepless men prescribe to wrest their minds from anxious and exciting preoccupations.

"Do you paint, sir?" asked Drayton, who was really interested.

"Bah! never. I can make just a little scratching with my pencil, enough to remind. But paint—oh—ha, ha, ha!—no. 'Tis an art I can admire; but should no more think to practise than the dance."

And the ponderous M. Varbarriere pointed his toe and made a mimic pirouette, snapped his fingers, and shrugged his round shoulders.

"Alas! sir, the more I appreciate the dance, the more I despair of figuring in the ballet, and so with painting. Perhaps, though, *you* paint?"

"Well, I just draw a little—what you call scratching, and I have tried a little tinting; but I'm sure it's very bad. I don't care about fools, of course, but I should be afraid to show it to anyone who knew anything about it—to you, for instance," said Drayton, who, though conceited, had sense enough at times to be a little modest.

"What is it?" said Miss Blunket, skipping into the hall, with a pretty little basket on her arm, and such a coquettish little hat on, looking so naïve and girlish, and so remarkably tattooed with wrinkles. "Shall I run away—is it a secret?"

"Oh, no; we have no secrets," said Drayton.

"No secrets," echoed Varbarriere.

"And won't you tell? I'm such a curious, foolish, wretched creature;" and she dropped her eyes like a flower-girl in a play.

What lessons, if we only could take them, are read us every hour! What a giant among liars is vanity! Here was this withered witch, with her baptismal registry and her looking-glass, dressing herself like a strawberry girl, and fancying herself charming!

"Only about my drawings—nothing."

"Ah, I know. Did Mr. Drayton show them to you?"

"No, Mademoiselle; I've not been so fortunate."

"He showed them to me, though. It's not any harm to tell, is it? and they really *are*—Well, I won't say all I think of them."

"I was just telling Monsieur Varbarriere, it is not everyone I'd show those drawings to. Was not I, Monsieur?" said Drayton, with a fine irony.

"So he was, upon my honour," said Varbarriere, gravely.

"He did not mean it, though," simpered Miss Blunket, "if *you* can't— *I*'ll try to induce him to show them to you; they are——Oh! here is Beatrix."

"How is your papa now, Mademoiselle?" asked Varbarriere, anxious to escape.

"Just as he was, I think, a little low, the Doctor says."

"Ah!" said Varbarriere, and still his dark eyes looked on hers with grave inquiry.

"He always *is* low for a day or two; but he says this will be nothing. He almost hopes to be down this evening."

"Ah! Yes. That's very well," commented Varbarriere, with pauses between, and his steady, clouded gaze unchanged.

"We are going to the garden; are you ready, darling?" said she to Miss Blunket.

"Oh, quite," and she skipped to the door, smiling this way and that, as she stood in the sun on the step. "Sweet day," and she looked back on Beatrix and the invitation, glanced slightly on Drayton, who looked loweringly after them unmoved, and thought—

"Why the plague does she spoil her walks with that frightful old humbug? There's no escaping that creature."

We have only conjecture as to which of the young ladies, now running down the steps, Mr. Drayton's pronouns referred to.

"You fish to-day?" asked Varbarriere, on whose hands time dragged strangely.

"We were thinking of going down to that pretty place Gryston. Linnett was there on Saturday morning. It was Linnett's trout you thought so good at luncheon."

And with such agreeable conversation they loitered a little at the door, and suddenly, with quick steps, there approached, and passed them by, an apparition.

It was old General Lennox. He had been walking in the park—about the grounds—he knew not where, since daybreak. Awfully stern he looked, fatigued, draggled he well might be, gloveless, one hand in his pocket, the other clenched on his thumb like a child's in a convulsion. His thoughts were set on something remote, for he brushed by the gentlemen, and not till he had passed did he seem to hear Drayton's cheery salutation, and stopping and turning towards them suddenly, he said, very grimly—

"Beg your pardon—"

"Nothing, General, only wishing you good-morning," answered Drayton.

"Yes, charming morning. I've been walking. I've been out—a— thank you," and that lead-coloured and white General vanished like a wicked ghost.

"'Gad, he looks as if he'd got a licking. Did you ever see a fellow look so queer?"

"He's been overworking his mind—business, you know—wants rest, I suspect," said Varbarriere, with a solemn nod.

"They say fellows make themselves mad that way. I wonder has he had any breakfast; did you see his trowsers all over mud?"

"I half envy your walk to Gryston," said Varbarriere, glancing up towards the fleecy clouds and blue sky, and down again to the breezy landscape. "It's worth looking at, a very pretty bit, that steep bridge and glen."

"No notion of coming; maybe you will?"

Varbarriere smiled and shook his head.

"No angler, sir, never was," he said.

"A bad day, rather, at all events," said Drayton; "a grey day is the thing for us."

"Ah, yes, a grey day; so my nephew tells me; a pretty good angler, I believe."

Varbarriere did not hear Drayton's answer, whatever it was; he was thinking of quite other things, and more and more feverishly every minute. The situation was for him all in darkness. But there remained on his mind the impression that something worse even than a guilty discovery had occurred last night, and the spectre that had just crossed them in the hall was not a sight to dissipate those awful shadows.

CHAPTER XXVII.

Lady Alice Redcliffe makes General Lennox's Acquaintance.

Old General Lennox stopped a servant on the stairs, and learned from the staring domestic where Lady Alice Redcliffe then was.

That sad and somewhat virulent old martyr was at that moment in her accustomed haunt, Lady Mary's boudoir, and in her wonted attitude over the fire, pondering in drowsy discontent over her many miseries, when a sharp knock at the door startled her nerves and awakened her temper.

Her "come in" sounded sharply, and she beheld for the first time in her life the General, a tall lean old man, with white bristles on brow and cheek, with his toilet disordered by long and rather rapid exercise, and grim and livid with no transient agitation.

"Lady Alice Redcliffe?" inquired he, with a stiff bow, remaining still inclined, his eyes still fixed on her.

"*I* am Lady Alice Redcliffe," returned that lady, haughtily, having quite forgotten General Lennox and all about him.

"My name is Lennox," he said.

"Oh, *General* Lennox? I was told you were here last night," said the old lady, scrutinising him with a sort of surprised frown; his dress and appearance were a little wild, and not in accordance with her ideas on military precision. "I am happy, General Lennox, to make your acquaintance. You've just arrived, I dare say?"

"I arrived yesterday—last night—last night late. I—I'm much obliged. May I say a word?"

"Certainly, General Lennox," acquiesced the old lady, looking harder at him—"certainly, but I must remind you that I have been a sad invalid, and therefore very little qualified to discuss or advise;" and she leaned back with a fatigued air, but a curious look nevertheless.

"I—I—it's about my wife, ma'am. We can—we can't live any longer together." He was twirling his gold eyeglass with trembling fingers as he spoke.

"You have been quarrelling—h'm?" said Lady Alice, still staring hard at him, and rising with more agility than one might have expected; and shutting the door, which the old General had left open, she said, "Sit down, sir—quarrelling, eh?"

"A quarrel, madam, that can never be made up—by ——, *never.*" The General smote his gouty hand furiously on the chimneypiece as he thus spake.

"Don't, General Lennox, *don't*, pray. If you can't command yourself, how can you hope to bear with one another's infirmities? A quarrel? H'm."

"Madam, we've separated. It's worse, ma'am—all over. I thought, Lady—Lady—I thought, madam, I might ask you, as the only early friend—a friend, ma'am, and a kinswoman—to take her with you for a little while, till some home is settled for her; *here* she can't stay, of course, an hour. That villain! May —— damn him."

"Who?" asked Lady Alice, with a kind of scowl, quite forgetting to rebuke him this time, her face darkening and turning very pale, for she saw it was another great family disgrace.

"Sir Jekyl Marlowe, ma'am, of Marlowe, Baronet, Member of Parliament, Deputy Lieutenant," bawled the old General, with shrill and trembling voice. "I'll drag him through the law courts, and the divorce court, and the House of Lords." He held his right fist up with its trembling knuckles working, as if he had them in Sir Jekyl's cravat, "drag him through them all, ma'am, till the dogs would not pick his bones; and I'll shoot him through the head, by ——, I'll shoot him through the head, and his family ashamed to put his name on his tombstone."

Lady Alice stood up, with a face so dismal it almost looked wicked.

"I see, sir; I see there's something very bad; I'm sorry, sir; I'm very sorry; I'm *very* sorry."

She had a hand of the old General's in each of hers, and was shaking them with a tremulous clasp.

Such as it was, it was the first touch of sympathy he had felt. The old General's grim face quivered and trembled, and he grasped *her* hands too, and then there came those convulsive croupy sobs, so dreadful to hear, and at last tears, and this dried and bleached old soldier wept loud and piteously. Outside the door you would not have known what to make of these cracked, convulsive sounds. You would have stopped in horror, and fancied some one dying. After a while he said—

"Oh! ma'am, I was very fond of her—I *was*, desperately. If I could know it was all a dream, I'd be content to die. I wish, ma'am, you'd advise me. I'll go back to India, I think; I could not stay here. You'll know best, madam, what she ought to do. I wish everything the best for her—you'll see, ma'am—you'll know best."

"Quite—quite; yes, these things are best settled by men of business. There are papers, I believe, drawn up, arranged by lawyers, and things, and I'm sorry, sir—"

And old Lady Alice suddenly began to sob.

"I'll—I'll do what I can for the poor thing," she said. "I'll take her to Wardlock—it's quite solitary—no prying people—and then to— perhaps it's better to go abroad; and you'll not make it public sooner than it must be; and it's a great blow to me, sir, a terrible blow. I wish she had placed herself more under direction; but it's vain looking back—she always refused advice, poor, poor wretched thing! Poor Jennie! We must be resigned, sir; and—and, sir, for

God's sake, no fighting—no pistoling. That sort of thing is never heard of now; and if you do, the whole world will be ringing with it, and the unfortunate creature the gaze of the public before she need be, and perhaps some great crime added—some one killed. Do you promise?"

"Ma'am, it's hard to promise."

"But you *must*, General Lennox, or I'll take measures to stop it this moment," cried Lady Alice, drying her eyes and glaring at him fiercely.

"Stop it! *who'll* stop it?" holloed the General with a stamp.

"*You'll* stop it, General," exclaimed the old lady; "your own common sense; your own compassion; your own self-respect; and not the less that a poor old woman that sympathises with you implores it."

There was here an interval.

"Ma'am, ma'am, it's not easy; but I will—I *will*, ma'am. I'll go this moment; I will, ma'am; I can't trust myself here. If I met him, ma'am, by Heaven I *couldn't*."

"Well, thank you, *thank* you, General Lennox—*do* go; there's not much chance of meeting, for he's ill; but go, don't stay a moment, and write to me to Wardlock, and you shall hear everything. There—go. Good-bye."

So the General was gone, and Lady Alice stood for a while bewildered, looking at the door through which he had vanished.

It is well when these sudden collapses of the overwrought nerves occur. More dejected, more broken, perhaps, he looked, but much more like the General Lennox whom his friends remembered. Something of the panic and fury of his calamity had subsided, too; and though the grief must, perhaps, always remain pretty much unchanged, yet he could now estimate the situation more justly, and take his measures more like a sane man.

In this better, if not happier mood, Varbarriere encountered him in that overshadowed back avenue which leads more directly than the main one to the little town of Marlowe.

Varbarriere was approaching the house, and judged, by the General's slower gait, that he was now more himself.

The large gentleman in the Germanesque felt hat raised that grotesque head-gear, French fashion, as Lennox drew nigh.

The General, with two fingers, made him a stern, military salute in reply, and came suddenly to a standstill.

"May I walk a little with you, General Lennox?" inquired Varbarriere.

"Certainly, sir. *Walk?* By all means; I'm going to London," rejoined the General, without, however, moving from the spot where he had halted.

"Rather a long stretch for me," thought Varbarriere, with one of those inward thrills of laughter which sometimes surprise us in the gravest moods and in the most unsuitable places. He looked sober enough, however, and merely said—

"You, know, General, there's some one ill up there," and he nodded mysteriously toward the house.

"Is there? Ay. Well, yes, I dare say," and he laughed with a sudden quaver. "I was not sure; the old woman said something. I'm glad, sir."

"I—I think I *know* what it is, sir," said Varbarriere.

"So do I, sir," said the General, with another short laugh.

"You recollect, General Lennox, what you promised me?"

"Ay, sir; how can I help it?" answered he.

"How can you help it! I don't quite see your meaning," replied Varbarriere, slowly. "I can only observe that it gives me new ideas of a soldier's estimate of his promise."

"Don't blame me, sir, if I lost my head a little, when I saw that villain there, in *my* room, sir, by ——" and the General cursed him here parenthetically through his clenched teeth; "I felt, sir, as—as if the sight of him struck me in the face—mad, sir, for a minute—I suppose, *mad*, sir; and—it occurred. I say, sir, I can't help it—and I couldn't help it, by —— I couldn't."

Varbarriere looked down with a peevish sneer on the grass and innocent daisies at his feet, his heel firmly placed, and tapping the sole of his boot from that pivot on the sward, like a man beating time to a slow movement in an overture.

"Very good, sir! It's your own affair. I suppose you've considered consequences, if anything should go wrong?"

And without awaiting an answer, he turned and slowly pursued his route toward the house. I don't suppose, in his then frame of mind, the General saw consequences very clearly, or cared about them, or was capable, when the image of Sir Jekyl presented itself, of any emotions but those of hatred and rage. He had gone now, at all events; the future darkness; the past irrevocable.

CHAPTER XXVIII.

The Bishop sees the Patient.

In the hall Varbarriere met the Reverend Dives Marlowe.

"Well, sir, how is Sir Jekyl?" asked he.

The parson looked bilious and lowering.

"To say truth, Monsieur, I can't very well make out what the Doctor thinks. I suspect he does not understand very well himself. *Gout*, he says, but in a very sinking state; and we've sent for the physician at Slowton; and altogether, sir, I'm very uneasy."

I suppose if the blow had fallen, the reverend gentleman would in a little while have become quite resigned, as became him. There were the baronetcy and some land; but on the whole, when Death drew near smirking, and offered on his tray, with a handsome black pall over it, these sparkling relics of the late Sir Jekyl Marlowe, Bart., the Rev. Dives turned away; and though he liked these things well enough, put them aside honestly, and even with a sort of disgust. For Jekyl, as I have said, though the brothers could sometimes exchange a sharp sally, had always been essentially kind to him; and Dives was not married, and, in fact, was funding money, and in no hurry; and those things were sure to come to him if he lived, sooner or later.

"And what, may I ask, do you suppose it *is*?" inquired Varbarriere.

"Well, *gout*, you know—he's positive; and, poor fellow, he's got it in his foot, and a very nasty thing it is, I know, even *there*. We all of us have it hereditarily—our family." The apostle and martyr did not want him to suppose he had earned it. "But I am very anxious, sir. Do *you* know anything of gout? May it be *there* and somewhere else at the same time? Two members of our family died of it in the stomach, and one in the head. It has been awfully fatal with us."

Varbarriere shook his head. He had never had a declared attack, and had no light to throw on the sombre prospect. The fact is, if that solemn gentleman had known for certain exactly how matters stood, and had not been expecting the arrival of his contumacious nephew, he would have been many miles on his way to London by this time.

"You know—you know, *sinking* seems very odd as a symptom of common gout in the great toe," said Dives, looking in his companion's face, and speaking rather like a man seeking than communicating information. "We must not frighten the ladies, you know; but I'm very much afraid of something in the stomach, eh? and possibly the heart."

"After all, sir," said Varbarriere, with a brisk effort, "Doctor—a—what's his name?—he's but a rural practitioner—an apothecary—is not it so?"

"The people here say, however, he's a very clever fellow, though," said Dives, not much comforted.

"We may hear a different story when the Slowton doctor comes. I venture to think we shall. I always fancied when gout was well out in the toe, the internal organs were safe. Oh! there's the Bishop."

"Just talking about poor Jekyl, my lord," said Dives, with a sad smile of deference, the best he could command.

"And—and how *is* my poor friend and pupil, Sir Jekyl?—better, I trust," responded the apostle in gaiters and apron.

"Well, my lord, we hope—I trust everything satisfactory; but the Doctor has been playing the sphinx with us, and I don't know exactly what to make of him."

"I saw Doctor Pratt for a moment, and expressed my wish to see his patient—my poor pupil—before I go, which must be—yes—within an hour," said the Bishop, consulting his punctual gold watch. "But he preferred my postponing until Doctor—I forget his name—very much concerned, *indeed*, that a second should be thought necessary—from Slowton—should have arrived. It—it gives me— I—I can't deny, a rather serious idea of it. Has he had many attacks?"

"Yes, my lord, several; never threatened seriously, but once—at Dartbroke, about two years ago—in the stomach."

"Ah! I forgot it was the stomach. I remember his illness though," said the Bishop, graciously.

"Not *actually* the stomach—only threatened," suggested Dives, deferentially. "I have made acquaintance with it myself, too, slightly; never so sharply as poor Jekyl. I *wish* that other doctor would come! But even at best it's not a pleasant visitor."

"I dare say—I can well suppose it. *I* have reason to be *very* thankful. I've *never* suffered. My poor *father* knew what it was—suffered horribly. I remember him at Buxton for it—horribly."

The Bishop was fond of this recollection, people said, and liked it to be understood that there was gout in the family, though he could not show that aristocratic gules himself.

At this moment Tomlinson approached, respectfully—I might even say religiously—and with such a reverence as High-Churchmen make at the creed, accosted the prelate, in low tones like distant organ-notes, murmuring Sir Jekyl's compliments to "his lordship, and would be very 'appy to see his lordship whenever it might be his convenience." To which his lordship assented, with a grave "*Now*, certainly, I shall be most happy," and turning to Dives—

"This, I hope, looks well. I fancy he must feel better. Let us hope;" and with slightly uplifted hand and eyes, the good Bishop followed Tomlinson, feeling so oddly as he threaded the same narrow half-lighted passages, whose corners and panelling came sharply on his memory as he passed them, and ascended the steep back stair with the narrow stained-glass slits, by which he had reached, thirty years ago, the sick-chamber of the dying Sir Harry Marlowe.

The Bishop sighed, looking round him, as he stood on the lobby outside the little ante-room. The light fell through the slim coloured orifice opposite on the oak before him, just as it did on the day he last stood there. The banisters, above and below, looked on him like yesterday's acquaintances; and the thoughtful frown of the heavy oak beams overhead seemed still knit over the same sad problem.

"*Thirty* years ago!" murmured the Bishop, with a sad smile, nodding his silvery head slightly, as his saddened eyes wandered over these things. "What is man that thou art mindful of him, or the son of man that thou so regardest him?"

Tomlinson, who had knocked at the Baronet's door, returned to say he begged his lordship would step in.

So with another sigh, peeping before him, he passed through the small room that interposed, and entered Sir Jekyl's, and took his hand very kindly and gravely, pressing it, and saying in the low tone which becomes a sick-chamber—

"I trust, my dear Sir Jekyl, you feel better."

"Thank you, pretty well; very good of you, my lord, to come. It's a long way, from the front of the house—a journey. He told me you were in the hall."

"Yes, it is a large house; interesting to me, too, from earlier recollections."

"You were in this room, a great many years ago, with my poor father. He died here, you know."

"I'm afraid you're distressing yourself speaking. Yes; oddly enough, I recognised the passages and back stairs; the windows, too, are peculiar. The *furniture*, though, that's changed—is not it?"

"So it is. I hated it," replied Sir Jekyl. "Balloon-hacked blue silk things—faded, you know. It's curious you should remember, after such a devil of a time—such a great number of years, my lord. I hated it. When I had that fever here in this room—thirteen— fourteen years ago—ay, by Jove, it's *fifteen*—they were going to write for *you*."

"Excuse me, my dear friend, but it seems to me you *are* exerting yourself too much," interposed the prelate again.

"Oh dear no! it does me good to talk. I had all sorts of queer visions. People fancy, you know, they see things; and I used to think I saw him—my poor father, I mean—every night. There were six of those confounded blue-backed chairs in this room, and a nasty idea got into my head. I had a servant—poor Lewis—then a very trustworthy fellow, and liked me, I think; and Lewis told me the doctors said there was to be a crisis on the night week of the first consultation— seven days, you know."

"I really fear, Sir Jekyl, you are distressing yourself," persisted the Bishop, who did not like the voluble eagerness and the apparent fatigue, nevertheless, with which he spoke.

"Oh! it's only a word more—it doesn't, I assure you—and I perceived he sat on a different chair, d'ye see, every night, and on the fourth night he had got on the fourth chair; and I liked his face less and less every night. You know he hated me about Molly— about *nothing*—he always hated me; and as there were only six chairs, it got into my head that he'd get up on my bed on the seventh, and that I should die in the crisis. So I put all the chairs out of the room. They thought I was raving; but I was quite right, for he did not come again, and here I am;" and with these words there came the rudiments of his accustomed chuckle, which died out in a second or two, seeming to give him pain.

"Now, you'll promise me not to talk so much at a time till you're better. I am glad, sir—very glad, Sir Jekyl, to have enjoyed your hospitality, and to have even this opportunity of thanking you for it. It is very delightful to me occasionally to find myself thus beholden to my old pupils. I have had the pleasure of spending a few days with the Marquis at Queen's Dykely; in fact, I came direct from him to you. You recollect him—Lord Elstowe he was then? You remember Elstowe at school?"

"To be sure; remember him very well. We did not agree, though—always thought him a cur," acquiesced Sir Jekyl.

The Bishop cleared his voice.

"He was asking for you, I assure you, very kindly—very kindly indeed, and seems to remember his school-days very affectionately, and—and pleasantly, and quite surprised me with his minute recollections of all the boys."

"They all hated him," murmured Sir Jekyl. "I did, I know."

"And—and I think we shall have a fine day. I drive always with two windows open—a window in front and one at the side," said the Bishop, whose mild and dignified eyes glanced at the windows, and the pleasant evidences of sunshine outside, as he spoke, "I was almost afraid I should have to start without the pleasure of saying good-bye. You remember the graceful farewell in Lucretius? I venture to say your brother does. I made your class recite it, do you remember?"

And the Bishop repeated three or four hexameters with a look of expectation at his old pupil, as if looking to him to take up the recitation.

"Yes, I am sure of it. I think I remember; but, egad! I've quite forgot my Latin, any I knew," answered the Baronet, who was totally unable to meet the invitation; "I—I don't know how it is, but I'm sorry you have to go to-day, very sorry;—sorry, of course, any time, but particularly I feel as if I should get well again very soon—that is, if you were to stay. Do you think you can?"

"Thank you, my dear Marlowe, thank you very much for that feeling," said the good Bishop, much gratified, and placing his old hand very kindly in that of the patient, just as Sir Jekyl suddenly remembered his doing once at his bedside in the sick-house in younger days, long ago, when he was a school-boy, and the Bishop master; and both paused for a moment in one of those dreams of the past that make us smile so sadly.

CHAPTER XXIX.

In the Yard of the Marlowe Arms.

The Bishop looked at his watch, and smiled, shaking his head.

"Time flies. I must, I fear, take my leave."

"Before you go," said Sir Jekyl, "I must tell you I've been thinking over my promise about that odious green chamber, and I'll pledge you my honour I'll fulfil it. I'll not leave a stone of it standing; I won't, I assure you. To the letter I'll fulfil it."

"I never doubted it, my dear Sir Jekyl."

"And must you really leave me to-day?"

"No choice, I regret."

"It's very unlucky. You can't think how your going affects me. It seems so odd and unlucky, so depressing just now. I'd have liked to talk to you, though I'm in no danger, and know it. I'd like to hear what's to be said, clergymen are generally so pompous and weak; and to be sure," he said, suddenly recollecting his brother, "there's Dives, who is neither—who is a good clergyman, and learned. I say so, of course, my lord, with submission to you; but still it isn't quite the same—you know the early association; and it makes me uncomfortable and out of spirits your going away. You don't think you could possibly postpone?"

"No, my dear friend, quite impossible; but I leave you—tell him I said so—in excellent hands; and I'm glad to add, that so far as I can learn you're by no means in a dying state."

The Bishop smiled.

"Oh! I know that," said Sir Jekyl, returning that cheerful expansion; "I know that very well, my Lord: a fellow always knows pretty well when he's in anything of a fix—I mean his life at all in question; it is not the least that, but a sort of feeling or fancy. What does Doctor Pratt say it *is*?"

"Oh! gout, as *I* understand."

"Ah! yes, I have had a good deal in my day. Do you think I could tempt you to return, maybe, when your business—this particular business, I mean—is over?"

The Bishop smiled and shook his head.

"I find business—mine at least—a very tropical plant; as fast as I head it down, it throws up a new growth. I was not half so hard worked, I do assure you, when I was better able to work, at the school, long ago. You haven't a notion what it is."

"Well, but you'll come back some time, not very far away?"

"Who knows?" smiled the Bishop. "It is always a temptation. I can say that truly. In the meantime, I shall expect to hear that you are much better. Young Marlowe—I mean Dives," and the Bishop laughed gently at the tenacity of his old school habits, "will let me hear; and so for the present, my dear Sir Jekyl, with many, many thanks for a very pleasant sojourn, and with all good wishes, I bid you farewell, and may God bless you."

So having shaken his hand, and kissing his own as he smiled another farewell at the door, the dignified and good prelate disappeared mildly from the room, Jekyl following him with his eyes, and sighing as the door closed on him.

As Sir Jekyl leaned back against his pillows, there arrived a little note, in a tall hand; some of the slim l's, b's, and so on, were a little spiral with the tremor of age.

"Lady Halice Redcliffe, Sir Jekyl, please sir, sends her compliments and hopes you may be able to read it, and will not leave for Warlock earlier than half-past one o'clock."

"Very well. Get away and wait in the outer room," said Sir Jekyl, flushing a little, and looking somehow annoyed.

"I hate the sight of her hand. It's sealed, too. I wish that cursed old woman was where she ought to be; and she chooses *now* because she knows I'm ill, and can't bear worry."

Sir Jekyl twirled the little note round in his fingers and thumb with a pinch. The feverish pain he was suffering did not improve his temper, and he was intemperately disposed to write across the back of the unopened note something to this effect:—"Ill and suffering; the pleasure of your note might be too much for me; pray keep it till to-morrow."

But curiosity and something of a dread that discovery had occurred prompted him to open it, and he read—

> "Having had a most painful interview with unhappy General Lennox, and endured mental agitation and excitement which are too much for my miserable health and nerves, I mean to return to Wardlock as early to-day as my strength will permit, taking with me, at his earnest request, *your victim.*"

"D—n her!" interposed Sir Jekyl through his set teeth.

> "I think you will see," he read on, "that this house is no longer a befitting residence for your poor innocent girl. As I am charged for a time with the care of the ruined wife of your friend and guest, you will equally see that it is quite impossible to offer my darling Beatrix an asylum at Wardlock. The Fentons, however, will, I am sure, be happy to receive her. She must leave Marlowe, of course, before I do. While here, she is under *my care*; but this house is no home for her; and you can hardly wish that *she* should be *sacrificed* in the ruin of the poor wife whom you have made an *outcast.*"

"Egad! it's the devil sent that fiend to torture me so. It's all about, I suppose," exclaimed Sir Jekyl, with a gasp. "Unlucky! The stupid old fribble, to think of his going off with his story to that Pharisaical old tattler!"

The remainder of the letter was brief.

> "I do not say, Jekyl Marlowe, that I regret your illness. You have to thank a merciful Providence that it is unattended with danger; and it affords an opportunity for reflection, which may, if properly improved, lead to some awakening of conscience— to a proper estimate of your past life, and an amendment of the space that remains. I need hardly add, that an amended life involves reparation, so far as practicable, to *all* whom you or, in your interest, *yours* may have injured.
>
> "In deep humiliation and sorrow,
>
> "Alice Redcliffe."
>
> "I wish you were in a deep pond, you plaguy old witch. That fellow, Herbert Strangways— Varbarriere—he's been talking to her. I know what she means by all that cant."

Then he read over again the passages about "your victim," and "General Lennox," your "friend and guest." And he knocked on the table, and called as well as he could—"Tomlinson," who entered.

"Where's General Lennox?"

"Can't say, Sir Jekyl, please, sir—'avn't saw him to-day."

"Just see, please, if he's in the house, and let him know that I'm ill, but very anxious to see him. You may say *very* ill, do you mind, and only wish a word or two."

Tomlinson bowed and disappeared.

"Don't care if he strikes me again. I've a word to say, and he *must* hear it," thought Sir Jekyl.

But Tomlinson returned with the intelligence that General Lennox had gone down to the town, and was going to Slowton station; and his man, with some of his things, followed him to the Marlowe Arms, in the town close by.

In a little while he called for paper, pen, and ink, and with some trouble wrote an odd note to old General Lennox.

"GENERAL LENNOX,

"You must hear me. By ——," and here followed an oath and an imprecation quite unnecessary to transcribe. "Your wife is innocent as an angel! I have been the fiend who would, if he could, have ruined her peace and yours. From your hand I have met my deserts. I lie now, I believe, on my death-bed. I wish you knew the whole story. The truth would deify her and make you happy. I am past the age of romance, though not of vice. I speak now as a dying man. I would not go out of the world with a perjury on my soul; and, by ——, I swear your wife is as guiltless as an angel. I am ill able to speak, but will see and satisfy you. Bring a Bible and a pistol with you—let me swear to every answer I make you; and if I have not convinced you before you leave, I promise to shoot myself through the head, and save you from all further trouble on account of

"JEKYL MARLOWE."

"Now see, Tomlinson, don't lose a moment. Send a fellow running, do you mind, and let him tell General Lennox I'm in pain—*very* ill— mind and—and all that; and get me an answer; and he'll put this in *his* hand."

Sir Jekyl was the sort of master who is obeyed. The town was hardly three-quarters of a mile away. His messenger accomplished the distance as if for a wager.

The waiter flourished his napkin in the hall of the Marlowe Arms, and told him—

"No General, *nothing* was there, as he heerd."

"Who do you want?" said the fat proprietress, with a red face and small eyes and a cap and satin bow, emerging from a side door, and superseding the waiter, who said—"A hofficer, isn't it?" as he went aside.

"Oh! from the Manor," continued the proprietress in a conciliatory strain, recognising the Marlowe button, though she did not know the man. "Can I do anything?"

And she instinctively dropped a courtesy—a deference to the far-off Baronet; and then indemnifying herself by a loftier tone to the menial.

"A note for General Lennox, ma'am."

"General Lennox?—I know, I think, a millentery man, white-'aired and spare?"

"I must give it 'im myself, ma'am, thankee," said he, declining the fat finger and thumb of the curious hostess, who tossed her false ringlets with a little fat frown, and whiffled—

"Here, tell him where's the tall, thin gemm'n, with white mistashes, that's ordered the hosses—that'll be him, I dessay," she said to the waiter, reinstated, and waddled away with a jingle of keys in her great pocket. So to the back yard they went, the thin, little, elderly waiter skipping in front, with a jerk or two of his napkin.

"Thankee, that's him," said the messenger.

CHAPTER XXX.

About Lady Jane.

The General was walking up and down the jolty pavement with a speed that seemed to have no object but to tire himself, his walking-stick very tightly grasped, his lips occasionally contracting, and his hat now and then making a vicious wag as he traversed his beat.

"Hollo!" said the General, drawing up suddenly, as the man stood before him with the letter, accosting him with his hand to his cap. "Hey! *well*, sir?"

"Letter, please, sir."

The General took it, stared at the man, I think, without seeing him, for a while, and then resumed his march, with his cane, sword-fashion, over his shoulder. The messenger waited, a little perplexed. It was not until he had made a third turn that the General, again observing the letter in his hand, looked at it, and again at the messenger, who was touching his cap, and stopping short, said—

"Well—ay! *This?*—aw—you *brought* it, didn't you?"

So the General broke it open—he had not his glasses with him—and, holding it far away, read a few lines with a dreadful glare, and then bursting all on a sudden into such a storm of oaths and curses as scared the sober walls of that unmilitary hostelry, he whirled his walking-stick in the air, with the fluttering letter extended toward the face of the astounded messenger, as if in another second he would sweep his head off.

At the sound of this hoarse screech the kitchen-wench looked open-mouthed out of the scullery-window with a plate dripping in her hand. "Boots," with his fist in a "Wellington," held his blacking-brush poised in air, and gazed also; and the hostler held the horse he was leading into the stable by the halter, and stood at the door gaping over his shoulder.

"Tell your master I said he may go to *hell*, sir," said the General, scrunching the letter like a snowball in his fist, and stamping in his fury.

What more he said I know not. The man withdrew, and, once or twice, turned about, sulkily, half puzzled and half angered, perhaps not quite sure whether he ought not to "lick" him.

"What'll be the matter now?" demanded the proprietress, looking from under her balustrade of brown ringlets from the back door.

"'Drat me if I know; he's a rum un, that he be," replied the man with the Marlowe button. "When master hears it he'll lay his whip across that old cove's shouthers, I'm thinking."

"I doubt he's not right in his head; he's bin a-walkin' up an' down the same way ever since he ordered the chaise, like a man beside himself. *Will* ye put *them* horses to?" she continued, raising her voice; "why, the 'arniss is on 'em this half-hour. Will ye put 'em to or *no*?" and so, in something of an angry panic, she urged on the preparations, and in a few minutes more General Lennox was clattering through the long street of the town, on his way to Slowton, and the London horrors of legal consultations, and the torture of the slow processes by which those whom God hath joined together are sundered.

"Send Donica Gwynn to me," said Lady Alice to the servant whom her bell had summoned to Lady Mary's boudoir.

When Donica arrived—

"Shut the door, Donica Gwynn," said she, "and listen. Come a little nearer, please. Sir Jekyl Marlowe is ill, and, of course, we cannot all stay here." Lady Alice looked at her dubiously.

"Fit o' the gout, my lady, I'm told."

"Yes, an attack of gout."

"It does not hold long with him, not like his poor father, Sir Harry, that would lie six months at a time in flannel. Sir Jekyl, law bless you, my lady! He's often 'ad his toe as red as fire overnight, and before supper to-morrow walking about the house. He says, Tomlinson tells me, this will be nothink at all; an' it might fret him sore, my lady, and bring on a worse fit, to see you all go away."

"Yes, very true, Gwynn; but there's something more at present," observed Lady Alice, demurely.

Donica folded her hands, and with curious eyes awaited her mistress's pleasure.

Lady Alice continued in a slightly altered tone—

"It's not altogether *that*. In fact, Gwynn, there has been—you're not to talk, d'ye see,—I know you *don't* talk; but there has been—there has been a *something*—a *quarrel*—between Lady Jane and her husband, the General; and for a time, at least, she will remain with me at Wardlock, and I may possibly go abroad with her for a little."

Donica Gwynn's pale sharp face grew paler and sharper, as during this announcement she eyed her mistress askance from her place near the door; and as Lady Alice concluded, Donica dropped her eyes to the Turkey carpet, and seemed to read uncomfortable mysteries in its blurred pattern. Then Donica looked up sharply, and asked—

"And, please, my lady, what is your ladyship's orders?"

"Well, Gwynn, you must get a 'fly' now from the town, and go on before us to Wardlock. We shall leave this probably in little more than an hour, in the carriage. Tell Lady Jane, with my compliments, that I hope she will be ready by that time—or no, you may give her my love—don't say compliments—and say, I will either go and see her in her room, or if she prefer, I will see her here, or anywhere else; and you can ask her what room at Wardlock she would like best—do you mind? Whatever room she would like best she shall have, except *mine*, of course, and the moment you get there you'll set about it."

"Yes, ma'am, please, my lady."

Donica looked at her mistress as if expecting something more; and her mistress looked away darkly, and said nothing.

"I'll return, my lady, I suppose, and tell you what Miss Jane says, ma'am?"

"Do," answered Lady Alice, and, closing her eyes, she made a sharp nod, which Donica knew was a signal of dismissal.

Old Gwynn, mounting the stairs, met Mrs. Sinnott with those keys of office which she had herself borne for so many years.

"Well, Mrs. Sinnott, ma'am, how's the master now?" she inquired.

"Doctor's not bin yet from Slowton, Mrs. Gwynn; we don't know nothink only just what you heard this morning from Mr. Tomlinson."

"Old Pratt, baint *he* here neither?"

"No, but the nurse be come."

"Oh! *respeckable*, I hope? But no ways, Mrs. Sinnott, ma'am, take my advice, and on no account don't you give her her will o' the bottle; there's none o' them hospital people but likes it—jest what's enough, and no more, I would say."

"Oh! no! no!" answered Mrs. Sinnott, scornfully. "I knows somethink o' them sort, too—leave 'em to me."

"Lady Alice going away this afternoon."

"And what for, Mrs. Gwynn?" asked the housekeeper.

"Sir Jekyl's gout."

"Fidgets! Tiresome old lass, baint she? law," said Mrs. Sinnott, who loved her not.

"She don't know Sir Jekyl's constitution like I does. Them little attacks o' gout, why he makes nothink o' them, and they goes and comes quite 'armless. I'm a-going back to Wardlock, Mrs. Sinnott, this morning, and many thanks for all civilities while 'ere, lest I should not see you when a-leavin'."

So with the housekeeper's smiles, and conventional courtesies, and shaking of hands, these ladies parted, and Mrs. Gwynn went on to the green chamber.

As she passed through the Window dressing-room her heart sank. She knew, as we are aware, a good deal about that green chamber, more than she had fancied Lady Jane suspected. She blamed herself for not having talked frankly of it last night. But Lady Jane's *éclat* of passion at one period of their interview had checked her upon any such theme; and after all, what could the green chamber have to do with it? Had not the General arrived express very late last night? It was some London story that sent him down from town in that hurry, and Sir Jekyl laid up in gout too. Some o' them jealous stories, and a quarrel over it. It will sure be made up again—ay, ay.

And so thinking, she knocked, and receiving no answer, she opened the door and peeped in. There was but a narrow strip of one shutter open.

"Miss Jennie, dear," she called. Still no answer. "Miss Jennie, darling." No answer still. She understood those sulky taciturnities well, in which feminine tempest sometimes subsides, and was not at all uneasy. On the floor, near the foot of the bed, lay the General's felt hat and travelling coat. Standing, there, she drew the curtain and saw Lady Jane, her face buried in the pillow, and her long hair lying wildly on the coverlet and hanging over the bedside.

"Miss Jennie, dear—Miss Jennie, darling; it's me—old Donnie, miss. Won't you speak to me?"

Still no answer, and Donica went round, beginning to feel uneasy, to the side where she lay.

CHAPTER XXXI.

Lady Jane's Toilet.

"Miss Jennie, *darling*, it's *me*," she repeated, and placed her fingers on the young lady's shoulder. It was with an odd sense of relief she saw the young lady turn her face away.

"Miss Jennie, dear; it's me—old Donnie—don't you know me?" cried Donica once more. "Miss, dear, my lady, what's the matter you should take on so?—only a few wry words—it will all be made up, dear."

"Who told you—who says it will be made up?" said Lady Jane, raising her head slowly, very pale, and, it seemed to old Gwynn, grown so thin in that one night. "Don't mind—it will *never* be made up—no, Donnie, never; it oughtn't. Is my—is General Lennox in the house?"

"Gone down to the town, miss, I'm told, in a bit of a tantrum—going off to Lunnon. It's the way wi' them all—off at a word; and then cools, and back again same as ever."

Lady Jane's fingers were picking at the bedclothes, and her features were sunk and peaked as those of a fever-stricken girl.

"The door is shut to—outer darkness. I asked your God for mercy last night, and see what he has done for me!"

"Come, Miss Jennie, dear, you'll be happy yet. Will ye come with me to Wardlock?"

"That I will, Donnie," she answered, with a sad alacrity, like a child's.

"I'll be going, then, in half an hour, and you'll come with me."

Lady Jane's tired wild eyes glanced on the gleam of light in the half-open shutter with the wavering despair of a captive.

"I wish we were there. I wish we were—you and I, Donnie—just you and I."

"Well, then, what's to hinder? My missus sends her love by me, to ask you to go there, till things be smooth again 'twixt you and your old man, which it won't be long, Miss Jennie, dear."

"I'll go," said Lady Jane, gliding out of her bed toward the toilet, fluttering along in her bare feet and night-dress. "Donnie, I'll go."

"That water's cold, miss; shall I fetch hot?"

"Don't mind—no; very nice. Oh, Donnie, Donnie, Donnie! my heart, my heart! what is it?"

"Nothink, my dear—nothink, darlin'."

"I wish it was dark again."

"Time enough, miss."

"That great sun shining! They'll all be staring. Well, *let* them."

"Won't you get your things on, darling? I'll dress you. You'll take cold."

"Oh, Donnie! I wish I could cry. My head! I don't know what it is. If I could cry I think I should be better. I must see him, Donnie."

"But he's gone away, miss."

"*Gone! Is* he?"

"Ay, sure I told ye so, dear, only this minute. To Lunnon, I hear say."

"Oh! yes, I forgot; yes, I'll dress. Let us make haste. I wish I knew. Oh! Donnie, Donnie! oh! my heart, Donnie, Donnie—my heart's breaking."

"There, miss, dear, don't take on so; you'll be better when we gets into the air, you will. What will ye put on?—here's a purple mornin' silk."

"Yes; very nice. Thank you. Oh! Donnie, I wish we were away."

"So we shall, miss, presently, please God. Them's precious bad pins—Binney and Clew—bends like lead; *there's* two on 'em. Thompson's mixed shillin' boxes—them's the best. Miss Trixie allays has 'em. Your hair's beautiful, miss, allays was; but dearie me! what a lot you've got! and so beautiful fine! I take it in handfuls— floss silk—and the weight of it! Beautiful hair, miss. Dearie me, what some 'id give for that!"

Thus old Gwynn ran on; but fixed, pale, and wild was the face which would once have kindled in the conscious pride of beauty at the honest admiration of old Donnie, who did not rise into raptures for everyone and on all themes, and whose eulogy was therefore valuable.

"I see, Donnie—nothing bad has happened?" said Lady Jane, with a scared glance at her face.

"Bad? Nonsense! I told you, Miss Jennie, 'twould all be made up, and so it will, please God, miss."

But Lady Jane seemed in no wise cheered by her promises, and after a silence of some minutes, she asked suddenly, with the same painful look—

"Donnie, tell me the truth, for God's sake; how is he?"

Donica looked at her with dark inquiry.

"The General is gone, you know, ma'am."

"*Stop*—you *know*," cried Lady Jane, seizing her fiercely by the arm, with a wild fixed stare in her face.

"Who?" said Donica.

"Not he. I mean—"

"Who?" repeated Gwynn.

"How is Sir Jekyl?"

It seemed as if old Donica's breath was suspended. Shade after shade her face darkened, as with wide eyes she stared in the gazing face of Lady Jane, who cried, with a strange laugh of rage—

"Yes—Sir Jekyl—how *is* he?"

"Oh, Miss Jane!—oh, Miss Jane!—oh, Miss Jane!—and is *that* it?"

Lady Jane's face was dark with other fiercer passions.

"Can't you answer, and not talk?" said she.

Donica's eyes wandered to the far end of the room to the fatal recess, and she was shaking her head, as if over a tale of horror.

"Yes, I see, you know it all, and you'll *hate* me now, as the others will, and I don't care."

Suspicions are one thing—faint, phantasmal; certainties quite another. Donica Gwynn looked appalled.

"Oh! poor Miss Jennie!" she cried at last, and burst into tears. Before this old domestic Lady Jane was standing—a statue of shame, of defiance—the fallen angelic.

"You're doing that to make me mad."

"Oh! no, miss; I'm sorry."

There was silence for a good while.

"The curse of God's upon this room," said Donica, fiercely, drying her eyes. "I wish you had never set foot in it. Come away, my lady. I'll go and send at once for a carriage to the town, and we'll go together, ma'am, to Wardlock. Shall I, ma'am?"

"Yes, I'll go," said Lady Jane. "Let us go, you and I. I won't go with Lady Alice. I won't go with her."

"Good-bye, my lady; good-bye, Miss Jennie dear; I'll be here again presently."

Dressed for the journey, with her cloak on and bonnet, Lady Jane sat in an arm-chair, haggard, listless, watching the slow shuffling of her own foot upon the floor, while Donica departed to complete the arrangements for their journey.

CHAPTER XXXII.

The two Doctors consult.

The doctor from Slowton had arrived at last. The horses, all smoking with the break-neck speed at which they had been driven, stood at the hall-door steps. The doctor himself, with Pratt and the nurse, were up-stairs in the patient's room. The Rev. Dives Marlowe, looking uncomfortable and bilious, hovered about the back stairs that led to Sir Jekyl's apartment, to waylay the doctors on their way down, and listened for the sound of their voices, to gather from their tones something of their spirits and opinions respecting his brother, about whose attack he had instinctive misgivings. The interview was a long one. Before it was over Dives had gradually ascended to the room outside the Baronet's, and was looking out of the window on the prospect below with the countenance with which one might look on a bad balance-sheet.

The door opened, the doctors emerged—the Slowton man first, Pratt following, both looking grave as men returning from the sacrament.

"Oh! Mr. Dives Marlowe—the Rev. Dives Marlowe," murmured Pratt as the door was shut.

The lean practitioner from Slowton bowed low, and the ceremony over—

"Well, gentlemen?" inquired the Rev. Dives Marlowe.

"We are about to compare notes, and discuss the case a little—Doctor Pratt and I—and we shall then, sir, be in a position to say something a—a—definite, we hope."

So the Rev. Dives withdrew to the stair-head, exchanging bows with the priests of Æsculapius, and there awaited the opening of the doors. When that event came, and the Rev. Dives entered—

"Well, Mr. Marlowe," murmured the Slowton doctor, a slight and dismal man of five-and-fifty—"we think, sir, that your brother, Sir Jekyl Marlowe, is not in immediate danger; but it would not be right or fair to conceal the fact that he is in a very critical state—highly so, in fact; and we think it better on the whole that some member of his family should advise him, if he has anything to arrange—a—a will, or any particular business, that he should see to it; and we think that—we are quite agreed upon this, Doctor Pratt?"

Pratt bowed assent, forgetful that he had not yet heard what they were agreed on.

"We think he should be kept very quiet; he's very low, and must have claret. We have told the nurse in what quantities to administer it, and some other things; she's a very intelligent woman, and your servants can take their directions from her."

Dives felt very oddly. We talk of Death all our lives, but know nothing about him until he stands in our safe homesteads suddenly before us, face to face. He is a much grizzlier object than we had fancied when busied with a brother or a child. What he is when he comes for ourselves, the few who have seen him waiting behind the doctor and live can vaguely remember.

"Good Lord, sir!" said Dives, "is he really in that state? I had no idea."

"Don't mis*take* us, sir. We don't say he may not, if everything goes right, do very well. Only the case is critical, and we should deceive you if we shrank from telling you so; is not that your view, Doctor—Dr. Pratt?"

Dr. Pratt was of course quite clear on the point.

"And you are in very able hands here," and the Slowton doctor waved his yellow fingers and vouchsafed a grave smile and nod of approbation toward Pratt, who wished to look indifferent under the compliment, but simpered a little in spite of himself.

The Rev. Dives Marlowe accompanied the two doctors down-stairs, looking like a man going to execution.

"You need not be afraid, sir," said Dives, laying his hand on the Slowton leech's sleeve. The grave gentleman stopped and inclined his ear to listen, and the three stood huddled together on the small landing, Dives' nervous fingers in the banister.

"I don't quite see, sir," observed the doctor.

"I give him up, sir; you need not be afraid to tell me."

"You are right, perhaps, to give him up; but I always say exactly what I think. Doctor—a—*Pratt* and I—we tell you frankly—we think him in a very critical state; but it's quite on the cards he may recover; and we have given very full directions to the nurse, who appears to be a very intelligent person; and don't let him shift his attitude unnecessarily, it may prejudice him, and be in fact attended with danger—very *serious* danger; and Doctor Pratt shall look in at five o'clock—you were so good as to say, Doctor Pratt, you would look in at five. Doctor Pratt will look in *then*, and do anything that may be necessary; and if there should be the slightest symptom of hæmorrhage send for him instantly, and the nurse knows what to do; and I think—I think I have said everything now."

"Hæmorrhage, sir! But *what* hæmorrhage? Why, what hæmorrhage is apprehended?" asked Dives, amazed.

"Internal or external it may occur," said the doctor; and Pratt, coughing and shaking his chops, interposed hurriedly and said—

"Yes, there may be a bleeding, it may come to that."

"He has bled a great deal already, you are aware," resumed the Slowton doctor, "and in his exhausted state a return of that might of course be very bad."

"But I don't understand," persisted Dives. "I beg pardon, but I really must. What *is* this hæmorrhage? it is not connected with gout, is it?"

"Gout, sir! no; who said gout? A bad wound, that seems to run toward the lung," answered the Slowton man.

"Wound! how's this? I did not hear," and Dives looked frightened, and inquiringly on Pratt, who said—

"Not hear, didn't you? Why, Sir Jekyl undertook to tell you, and would not let me. He took me in for a while, poor fellow, quite, and said 'twas gout, that's all. I'm surprised he did not tell you."

"No—*no*—not a word; and—and you think, sir, it may begin bleeding afresh?"

"That's what we chiefly apprehend. Farewell, sir. I find I have not a moment. I must be at Todmore in three quarters of an hour. A sad case that at Todmore; only a question of a few days, I'm afraid; and a very fine young fellow."

"Yes," said Dives—"I—I—it takes me by surprise. Pray, Dr. Pratt, don't go for a moment," and he placed his hand on his arm.

"Farewell, sir," said the Slowton doctor, and putting up his large gold watch, and bowing gravely, he ran at a quiet trot down the stairs, and jumped into his chaise at the back entrance, and vanished.

"You did not tell me," began Dives.

"No," said Pratt, promptly, "he said he'd tell *himself*, and did not choose me."

"And you think—you think it's very bad?"

"Very bad, sir."

"And you think he'll not get over it?"

"He may not, sir."

"It's frightful, Doctor, frightful. And how was it, do you know?"

"No more than the man in the moon. You must not tease him with questions, mind, to-day. In a day or two you may ask him. But he said, upon his honour, no one was to blame but himself."

"Merciful Heavens! sir. To think of his going this way!"

"Very sad, sir. But we'll do all we can, and possibly may pull him through."

With slow steps Dives began to ascend the stairs toward his brother's room. He recollected that he had not bid Pratt good-bye, and gave him his adieux over the banister; and then, with slow and creaking steps, mounted, and paused on the lobby, to let his head clear and to think how he should accost him.

Dives was not a Churchman to pester people impertinently about their sins; and out of the pulpit, where he lashed the vice but spared the man, he was a well-bred divine, and could talk of sheep, and even of horses, and read everything from St. Paul to Paul de Kock; and had ridden till lately after the hounds, and gave *recherché* little dinners, such as the New Testament character whose name, with a difference in pronunciation, he inherited might have praised, and well-iced champagne, which, in his present uncomfortable state, that fallen gentleman would have relished. And now he stood in a sombre mood, with something of panic at the bottom of it, frightened that the ice upon which men held Vanity Fair, and roasted oxen, and piped and danced, and gamed, should prove so thin; and amazed to see his brother drowning among the fragments in that black pool, and no one minding, and he unable to help him.

And it came to him like a blow and a spasm. "The special minister of Christ!—am I what I'm sworn to be? Can I go in and talk to him of those things that concern eternity with any effect? Will he mind me? Can I even now feel the hope, and lead the prayer as I ought to do?"

And Dives, in a sort of horror, as from the pit, lifted up his eyes, and prayed "have mercy on me!" and saw a misspent hollow life behind, and judgment before him; and blamed himself, too, for poor Jekyl, and felt something of the anguish of his namesake in the parable, and yearned for the safety of his brother.

Dives, in fact, was frightened for himself and for Jekyl, and in those few moments, on the lobby, his sins looked gigantic and the vast future all dismay; and he felt that, bad as poor Jekyl might be, *he* was worse—a false soldier—a Simon Magus—chaff, to be burnt up with unquenchable fire!

"I wish to God the Bishop had stayed over this night," said Dives, with clasped hands, and again turning his eyes upward. "We must send after him. I'll write to implore of him. Oh, yes, he'll come."

Even in this was a sense of relief; and treading more carefully, he softly turned the handle of the outer door, and listened, and heard Jekyl's cheerful voice say a few words to the nurse. He sighed with a sense of relief, and calling up a sunnier look, he knocked at Jekyl's half-open door, and stepped to his bedside.

CHAPTER XXXIII.

Varbarriere in the Sick-room.

"Well, Jekyl, my dear fellow—and how do you feel now? There, don't; you must not move, they told me," said Dives, taking his brother's hand, and looking with very anxious eyes in his face, while he managed his best smile.

"Pretty well—nothing. Have they been talking? What do they say?" asked Sir Jekyl.

"Say? Well, not much; those fellows never do; but they expect to have you all right again, if you'll just do what you're bid, in a week or two."

"Pratt's coming at five," he said. "What is it now?"

Dives held his watch to Jekyl, who nodded.

"Do you think I'll get over it, Dives?" he asked at length, rather ruefully.

"Get over? To be sure you will," answered Dives, doing his best. "It might be better for you, my dear Jekyl, if it *were* a little more serious. We all need to be pulled up a little now and then. And there's nothing like an alarm of—of that kind for making a man think a little; for, after all, health is only a long day, and a recovery but a reprieve. The sentence stands against us, and we must, sooner or later, submit."

"Yes, to be sure. We're all mortal, Dives—is not that your discovery?" said Sir Jekyl.

"A discovery it is, my dear fellow, smile as we may—a discovery to me, and to you, and to all—whenever the truth, in its full force, opens on our minds."

"That's when we're going to die, I suppose," said Sir Jekyl.

"*Then*, of course; but often, in the mercy of God, long before it. That, in fact, is what we call people's growing serious, or religious; their perceiving, as a fact, that they *are* mortal, and resolving to make the best preparation they can for the journey."

"Come, Dives, haven't those fellows been talking of me—eh?—as if I were worse than you say?" asked the Baronet, oddly.

"The doctors, you mean? They said exactly what I told you. But it is not, my dear Jekyl, when we are sick and frightened, and maybe despairing, that these things are best thought on; but when we are, like you and me, likely to live and enjoy life—*then* is the time. I've been thinking myself, my dear Jekyl, a good deal for some time past. I have been living too much in the spirit of the world; but I hope to do better."

"To do better—to be sure. You've always been hoping to do better; and I've given you a lift or two," said the Baronet, who, in truth, never much affected his brother's pulpit-talk, as he called it, and was falling into his old cynical vein.

"But, seriously, my dear fellow, I do. My mind has been troubled thinking how unworthy I have been of my calling, and how fruitless have been my opportunities, my dear brother, with you. I've never improved them; and I'd be so glad—now we are likely to have a few quiet days—if you'll let me read a little with you."

"Sermons, do you mean?" interposed the Baronet.

"Well, what's better?—a little of the Bible?"

"Come now, Dives, those doctors *have* been shaking their heads over me. I say, you must tell me. Do they say I'm in a bad way?"

"They think you'll recover."

"Did they tell you what it is?"

"Yes. A wound."

"They had no business, d—— them," said Sir Jekyl, flushing.

"Don't, don't, my dear Jekyl; they could not help it. I pressed that doctor—I forget his name—and he really could not help saying."

"Well, well, it doesn't much signify; I'd have told you myself by-and-by. But you must not tell—I've a reason—you must not tell anyone, mind. It was my fault, and I'm greatly to blame; and I'll tell you in a little while—a day or two—all about it."

"Yes, so you can. But, my dear Jekyl, you look much fatigued; you are exerting yourself."

Here the nurse interposed with the claret-jug, and intimated that the Rev. Dives was making her patient feverish, and indeed there was an unpleasantly hot hectic in each cheek. But the Baronet had no notion of putting himself under the command of the supernumerary, and being a contumacious and troublesome patient, told her to sit in the study and leave him alone.

"I've a word to say, Dives. I must see that fellow Herbert Strangways."

"*Who?*" said Dives, a good deal alarmed, for he feared that his brother's mind was wandering.

"Herbert—that fellow Varbarriere. I forgot I had not told you. Herbert Strangways, you remember; they're the same. And I want to see him. Better now than to-morrow. I may be feverish then."

"By Jove! It's very surprising. Do you really mean—"

"Yes; he is. I do; they are the same. You remember Herbert, of course—Herbert Strangways—the fellow I had that long chase after all over Europe. He has things to complain of, you know, and we might as well square the account in a friendlier way, eh?—don't you think?"

"And was it he—was there any altercation?" stammered Dives.

"That did *this*, you mean," said Sir Jekyl, moving his hand toward the wound. "Not a bit—no. He seems reasonable; and I should like—you know they are very old blood, and there's nothing against it—that all should be made up. And if that young fellow and Beatrix—don't you see? Is Tomlinson there?"

"In the outer room," said Dives.

"Call him. Tomlinson, I say, you take my compliments to Monsieur Varbarriere, and say, if he has no objection to see me for a few minutes here, I should be very happy. Try and make him out, and bring me word."

So Tomlinson disappeared.

"And, Dives, it tires me;—so will you—I'm sure you will—see Pelter, after we've spoken with that fellow Herbert, and consult what we had best do, you know. I dare say the young people would come to like one another—he's a fine young fellow; and that, you know, would be the natural way of settling it—better than law or fighting."

"A great deal—a great deal, certainly."

"And you may tell him I have that thing—the deed, you know—my poor father—"

"I—I always told you, my dear Jekyl, I'd rather know nothing of all that—in fact, I *do* know nothing; and I should not like to speak to Pelter on that subject. You can, another time, you know," said Dives.

"Well, it's in the red trunk in there."

"Pray, dear Jekyl, don't—I assure you I'd rather know nothing—I—I can't; and Pelter will understand you better when he sees you. But I'll talk to him with pleasure about the other thing, and I quite agree with you that any reasonable arrangement is better than litigation."

"Very well, be it so," said Sir Jekyl, very tired.

"I'm always drinking claret now—give me some—the only quick way of making blood—I've lost a lot."

"And you must not talk so much, Jekyl," said Dives, as he placed the glass at his lips; "you'll wear yourself out."

"Yes, I *am* tired," said the Baronet; "I'll rest till Strangways comes."

And he closed his eyes, and was quiet for a time. And Dives, leaning back in his chair at the bedside, felt better assured of Jekyl's recovery, and his thoughts began to return to their wonted channel, and he entertained himself with listlessly reading and half understanding a tedious sculling match in a very old copy of "Bell's Life," which happened to lie near him.

A tap at the outer door called up Dives from Sandy Dick's sweep round a corner, and Jekyl said—

"Tell him to come in—and stay—you're not to say I'm hurt—do you mind?"

"My dear Jekyl, I—I shan't say anything. There he's knocking again."

"Well, tell him—come in!"

"Come in!" echoed Dives, in a louder key.

And Monsieur Varbarriere entered with that mysterious countenance and cautious shuffle with which men enter a sick-chamber.

"Very sorry to hear you've been suffering," began Varbarriere, in a low tone.

"Thanks—you're very good, I'm sure," said Sir Jekyl, with a faint smile. "I—I wished very much to see you. I expect to be better very soon, and I thought I might have a word, as you are so good, in the meantime."

"Very happy, indeed—most happy, as long as you please; but you must not try too much. You know they say you may disturb gout if you try too much, particularly at first," said Varbarriere, knowing very well how little gout really had to do with it.

"Oh! no danger—doing very nicely," said Sir Jekyl.

"That's well—that's very good," said Varbarriere, with a leisurely sympathy, looking on him all the time, and calling to mind how the Comte de Vigny looked after he received the sword-thrust of which he died in Varbarriere's house, to which he had been carried after his duel with young D'Harnois. And he came to the conclusion that Sir Jekyl looked a great deal better than the Comte had done—and, in fact, that he would do very well.

CHAPTER XXXIV.

Guy Deverell arrives.

"Sit down, Herbert, I shan't keep you long. *There*, I've just been saying to Dives I think it's a pity we should quarrel any more—that is, if we can help it; and I don't see why we should not be friendly— I mean more friendly than, in fact, we have ever been—I don't; do you?"

"Why, I see no reason—none; that is, of course, with the reservations that are—that are always assumed—I don't see any."

Varbarriere was answering plausibly, politely, smiling. But it was not like last night, when for a few transient moments he had seemed moved from his equilibrium. There was no emotion now. It was diplomatic benignity. Still it was something. Here was his foe willing to hear reason.

"It was just in my mind—Dives and I talking—I think I've seen some signs of liking between the young people—I mean your nephew and Beatrix."

"Indeed!" interrupted Varbarriere, prolonging the last syllable after his wont, and raising his thick eyebrows in very naturally acted wonder.

"Well, yes—only a sort of conjecture, you know—haven't you?"

"Well, I—ha, ha! If I ever observed anything, it hasn't remained in my mind. But she is so lovely—Miss Marlowe—that I should not wonder. And you think—"

"I think," said Sir Jekyl, supplying the pause, "if it be so, we ought not to stand in the way; and here's Dives, who thinks so too."

"I—in fact, my brother, Jekyl, mentioned it, of course, to me—it would be a very happy mode of—of making matters—a—*happy*;

and—and that, I think, was all that passed," said Dives, thus unexpectedly called into the debate.

"This view comes on me quite by surprise. That the young fellow should adore at such a shrine is but to suppose him mortal," said Varbarriere, with something of his French air. "But—but you know the young lady—that's quite another thing—quite. Young ladies, you know, are not won all in a moment."

"No, of course. We are so far all in the clouds. But I wished to say so much to you; and I prefer talking face to face, in a friendly way, to sending messages through an attorney."

"A thousand thanks. I value the confidence, I assure you—yes, much better—quite right. And—and I shall be taking my leave to-morrow morning—business, my dear Sir Jekyl—and *greatly* regret it; but I've outstayed my time very considerably."

"Very sorry too—and only too happy if you could prolong it a little. *Could* you, do you think?"

Varbarriere shook his head, and thanked him with a grave smile again—but it was impossible.

"It is a matter—such an arrangement, should it turn out practicable—on which we should reflect and perhaps consult a little. It sounds not unpromisingly, however; we can talk again perhaps, if you allow it, before I go."

"So we can—you won't forget, and I shall expect to see you often and soon, mind."

And so for the present they parted, Dives politely seeing him to the head of the stairs.

"I think he entertains it," said Sir Jekyl to his brother.

"Yes, certainly, he does—yes, he entertains it. But I suspect he's a cunning fellow, and you'll want all the help you can get, Jekyl, if it comes to settling a bargain."

"I dare say," said Sir Jekyl, very tired.

Meanwhile our friend Varbarriere was passing through the conservatory, the outer door of which stood open ever so little, tempering the warmth of its artificial atmosphere. He stopped before a file of late exotics, looking at them with a grave meaning smile, and smelling at them abstractedly.

"Can the Ethiopian change his skin, or the leopard his spots? Selfish rogue! Could it be? A wedding, in which Guy, the son of that murdered friend, should act bridegroom, and the daughter of his murderer, bride; while he, the murderer, stood by smiling, and I, the witness, cried 'Amen' to the blessing! *Disgusting!* Never, *never*— bah! The proposition shows weakness. Good—*very* good! A come-down for you, Master Jekyl, when you sue for an alliance with Herbert Strangways! Oh! ho! ho! *Never!*"

A little while later, Varbarriere, who was standing at the hall-door steps, saw a chaise approaching. He felt a presentiment of what was coming. It pulled up at the door.

"No melodrama—no *fracas*—no foolery. Those young turkeys, my faith! they will be turkeys still. Here he comes, the hero of the piece! Well, what does it matter?" This was not articulated, spoken only in thought, and aloud he said—

"Ha!—Guy?"

And the young man was on the ground in a moment, pale and sad, and hesitated deferentially, not knowing how his uncle might receive him.

"So, here you are," said Varbarriere, coolly but not ill-humouredly. "Those rambles of yours are not much to the purpose, my friend, and cost some money—don't you see?"

Guy bowed sadly, and looked, Varbarriere saw, really distressed.

"Well, never mind—the expense need not trouble us," said Varbarriere, carelessly extending his hand, which Guy took. "We may be very good friends in a moderate way; and I'm not sorry you came, on the whole. Don't mind going in for a few minutes—you're very well—and let us come this way for a little."

So side by side they turned the corner of the house, and paced up and down the broad quiet walk under the windows.

"We must leave this immediately, Guy, Sir Jekyl is ill—more seriously I believe, than they fancy; not dangerously, but still a tedious thing. They call it gout, but I believe there is something more."

"Indeed! How sudden!" exclaimed Guy. And to do him justice, he seemed both shocked and sad, although perhaps all his sorrow was not on Sir Jekyl's account.

"And I'll be frank with you, Guy," continued Varbarriere. "I think I can see plainly, maybe, what has drawn you here. It is not I—it is not business—it is not Sir Jekyl. Who or what can it be?"

"I—I thought, sir, my letter had explained."

"And I am going away in the morning—and some of the party probably to-day; for there's no chance of Sir Jekyl's coming down for some time," continued Varbarriere, not seeming to hear Guy's interruptions.

"*Very* sorry!" said Guy, sincerely, and his eyes glanced along the empty windows.

"And so, you see, this visit here leads pretty much to nothing," continued Varbarriere. "And it might be best to keep that carriage for a few minutes—eh?—and get into it, and drive back again to Slowton."

"Immediately, sir?"

"Immediately—yes. I'll join you there in the morning, and we can talk over your plans then. I do not know exactly—we must consider. I don't want to part in unkindness. I wish to give you a lift, Guy, if you'll let me." So said Varbarriere in his off-hand way.

Guy bowed deferentially.

"And see, nephew; there's a thing—*attend*, if you please," said Varbarriere, lowering his voice.

"I attend, sir."

"See—you answer upon your honour—do you hear?"

"I do, sir. You hear nothing but truth from me."

"Well, yes—very good. Is there—have you any correspondence in this house?" demanded the ponderous uncle, and his full dark eyes turned suddenly on the young man.

"No, sir, no correspondence."

"No one writes to you?"

"No, sir."

"Nor you to anyone?"

"No, sir."

"There must be no nonsense of that kind, Guy—I've told you so before—put it quite out of your head. You need not speak—I am merely discussing a hypothesis—quite out of your head. Nothing could ever come of it but annoyance. You know, of course, to whom all this relates; and I tell you it can't be. There are reasons you shall hear elsewhere, which are final."

What Guy might have answered does not appear, for at that moment old Doocey joined them.

"Oh! come back—how d'ye do?—going to break up here, I fancy;" this was to Varbarriere; "Sir Jekyl's in for a regular fit of it evidently. Old Sir Paul Blunket was talking to Pratt, their doctor here—and old fellows, you know, go into particulars" (Doocey, of course, was rather a young fellow), "and generally know more about things of this sort—and he says Dr. Pratt thinks he'll not be on his legs for a month, egad. So he says he's going either to-night or to-morrow—and I'm off this evening; so is Linnett. Can I do anything for you at Llandudno? Going there first, and I want to see a little of North Wales before the season grows too late."

Varbarriere was grateful, but had nothing to transmit to Llandudno.

"And—and Drayton—*he's* going to stay," and he looked very sly. "An attraction, you know, *there*; besides, I believe he's related—is not he?—and, of course, old Lady Alice Redcliffe stays for chaperon. A great chance for Drayton."

There was a young man at his elbow who thought Doocey the greatest coxcomb and fool on earth, except, perhaps, Drayton, and who suffered acutely and in silence under his talk.

"Drayton's very spoony on her—eh?—the young lady, Miss Marlowe—haven't you observed?" murmured old Doocey, with a sly smile, to Varbarriere.

"Very suitable it would be—fine estate, I'm told," answered Varbarriere; "and a good-looking young fellow too."

"A—*rather*," acquiesced Doocey. "The kind of fellow that pays very well in a ball-room; he's got a lot to say for himself."

"And good family," contributed Varbarriere, who was not sorry that old Doocey should go on lowering his extinguisher on Guy's foolish flame.

"Well—well—*family*, you know—there's nothing very much of that—they—they—there was—it's not the family name, you know. But no one minds family now—all money—*we*'re a devilish deal better family, and so is Mr. Strangways here—all to nothing. I was telling him the other day who the Draytons are."

Precisely at this moment, through a half-open upper window, there issued a sudden cry, followed by sobs and women's gabble.

All stopped short—silent, and looking up—

"Some one crying," exclaimed Doocey, in an under-key.

And they listened again.

"Nothing bad, I hope," muttered Varbarriere, anxiously looking up like the rest.

A maid came to the window to raise the sash higher, but paused, seeing them.

"Come away, I say—hadn't we better?" whispered Doocey.

"Let's go in and ask how he is," suggested Varbarriere suddenly, and toward the hall-door they walked.

Was it something in the tone and cadence of this cry that made each in that party of three feel that a dreadful tragedy was consummated? I can't say—only they walked faster than usual, and in silence, like men anticipating evil news and hastening to a revelation.

CHAPTER XXXV.

I am Thine and Thou art Mine, Body and Soul, for ever.

In order to understand the meaning of this cry, it will be necessary to mention that so soon as the corpulent and sombre visitor had left the bed-room of Sir Jekyl Marlowe, Dives lent his reverend aid to the nurse in adjusting his brother more comfortably in his bed; and he, like Varbarriere, took instinctively a comfortable and confident view of Sir Jekyl's case, so that when the officious handmaid of Æsculapius assumed her airs of direction he put aside her interference rather shortly. At all events, there was abundance of time to grow alarmed in, and certainly no need for panic just now. So Dives took his leave for the present, the Baronet having agreed with him that his visitors had better be allowed to disperse to their own homes, a disposition to do so having manifested itself here and there among them.

Sir Jekyl, a little more easy in consequence of these manipulations, was lying back on pillows, with that pleasant confidence in his case at which a sanguine man so easily arrives, and already beginning to amuse himself with pictures in the uncertain future. The hospital nurse, sitting by a fire in that dim and faded study which opened from the sick-room, now and then rose, and with soundless steps drew near the half-open door, and sometimes peeped, and sometimes only listened. The patient was quiet. The woman sat down in that drowsy light, and ruminated, looking into the fire, with her feet on the fender, and a good deal of stocking disclosed; when, all on a sudden, she heard a rustling of a loose dress near her, and looking over her shoulder, surprised, still more so, saw a pale and handsome lady cross the floor from near the window to the door of Sir Jekyl's room, which she closed as she entered it.

With her mouth open, the nurse stood up and gazed in the direction in which she had disappeared. Sir Jekyl, on the other hand, witnessed her entrance with a silent amazement, scarcely less than the nurse's. A few hurried steps brought her to his bedside, and looking down upon him with great agony, and her hands clasped together, she said, with a kind of sob—

"Thank God, thank God!—alive, alive! Oh, Jekyl, what hours of torture!"

"Alive! to be sure I'm alive, little fool!" said the Baronet, with an effort, smiling uncomfortably. "They have not been telling you it's anything serious?"

"They told me nothing. I've heard nothing. I've seen no one but Gwynn. Oh, Jekyl! tell me the truth; what do they say?—there's so much blood on the floor."

"Why, my precious child, don't worry yourself about it; they evidently think it's nothing at all. I know it's nothing, only what they call, just, the muscles—you know—a little sore. I'll be on my legs again in a week."

"I'm going to Wardlock, Jekyl; you'll hear news of me from there."

Had the tone or the look something ineffably ominous? I know not.

"Come, Jennie, none of that," he answered. "No folly. I've behaved very badly. *I*'ve been to blame; altogether *my* fault. Don't tease yourself about what can't be helped. We must not do anything foolish, though. I'm tired of the world; so are you, Jennie; we are both sick of it. If we choose to live out of it, what the plague do we really lose?"

At this moment the nurse, slowly opening the door a little, said, with a look of quiet authority—

"Please, sir, the doctor said particular you were not to talk, sir."

"D—n you and the doctor—get out of that, and shut the door!" cried the Baronet; and the woman vanished, scared.

"Give me your hand, Jennie darling, and don't look as if the sky had fallen. I'm not going to make my bow yet, I promise you."

"And then, I suppose, a duel," said Lady Jane, wringing her hands in an agony.

"Duel, you little fool! Why, there's no such thing now, that is, in these countries. Put fighting quite out of your head, and listen to me. You're right to keep quiet for a little time, and Wardlock is as good a place as any. I shall be all right again in a few days."

"I can look no one in the face; no—never again—and Beatrix; and—oh, Jekyl, how will it be? I am half wild."

"To be sure, everyone's half wild when an accident happens, till they find it really does not signify two pence. Can't you listen to me, and not run from one thing to another? and I'll tell you everything."

With a trembling hand he poured some claret into a tumbler and drank it off, and was stronger.

"He'll take steps, you know, and I'll help all I can; and when you're at liberty, by—I'll marry you, Jane, if you'll accept me. Upon my honour and soul, Jennie, I'll do exactly whatever you like. *Don't* look so. *What* frightens you? I tell you we'll be happier than you can think or imagine."

Lady Jane was crying wildly and bitterly.

"Fifty times happier than ever we could have been if this—this annoyance had not happened. We'll travel. I'll lay myself out to please you, every way, and make you happy; upon my soul I will, Jennie. I owe you everything I can do. We'll travel. We'll not try pharisaical England, but abroad, where people have common sense. Don't, don't go on crying, darling, that way; you can't hear me; and there's really nothing to tease yourself about—quite the contrary, you'll see; you'll like the people abroad much better than here—more common sense and good nature; positively better people, and a devilish deal more agreeable and—and cleverer. And why do you go on crying, Jennie? You must not; hang it! you'll put me in the dumps. You don't seem to hear me."

"Yes, I do, I do; but it's all over, Jekyl, and I've come to bid you farewell, and on earth we'll never meet again," said Lady Jane, still weeping violently.

"Come, little Jennie, you shan't talk like a fool. I've heard you long enough; you must listen to me—I have more to say."

"Jekyl, Jekyl, I am sorry—oh! I'm sorry, for your sake, and for mine, I ever saw your face, and sorrier that I am to see you no more; but I've quite made up my mind—nothing shall change me—nothing—never. Good-bye, Jekyl. God forgive us. God bless you."

"Come, Jane, I say, don't talk that way. What do you mean?" said the Baronet, holding her hand fast in his, and with his other hand encircling her wrist. "If you really do want to make me ill, Jennie, you'll talk in that strain. I know, of course, I've been very much to blame. It was all my fault, I said—I *say*—everything; but now you will be free, Jennie. I wish I had been worthy of you; I wish I had. No, you must not go. Wait a moment. I say, Jennie, I wish to Heaven I had made you marry me when you might; but I'll not let you go now; by Heaven, I'll never run a risk of losing you again."

"No, Jekyl, no, I've made up my mind; it is all no use, I'll go. It is all over—quite over, for ever. Good-bye, Jekyl. God bless you. You'll be happier when we have parted—in a few days—a great deal happier; and as for me, I think I'm broken-hearted."

"By ——, Jennie, you shan't go. I'll make you swear; you shall be my wife—by Heaven, you shall; we'll live and die together. You'll be happier than ever you were; we have years of happiness. I'll be whatever you like. I'll go to church—I'll be a Puseyite, or a Papist, or anything you like best. I'll—I'll—"

And with these words Sir Jekyl let go her hand suddenly, and with a groping motion in the air, dropped back on the pillows. Lady Jane cried wildly for help, and tried to raise him. The nurse was at her side, she knew not how. In ran Tomlinson, who, without waiting for directions, dashed water in his face. Sir Jekyl lay still, with waxen face, and a fixed deepening stare.

"Looks awful bad!" said Tomlinson, gazing down upon him.

"The wine—the claret!" cried the woman, as she propped him under the head.

"My God! what is it?" said Lady Jane, with white lips.

The woman made no answer, but rather shouldered her, as she herself held the decanter to his mouth; and they could hear the glass clinking on his teeth as her hand trembled, and the claret flowed over his still lips and down upon his throat.

"Lower his head," said the nurse; and she wiped his shining forehead with his handkerchief; and all three stared in his face, pale and stern.

"Call the doctor," at last exclaimed the nurse. "He's not right."

"Doctor's gone, I think," said Tomlinson, still gaping on his master.

"*Send* for him, *man*! I tell ye," cried the nurse, scarce taking her eyes from the Baronet.

Tomlinson disappeared.

"Is he better?" asked Lady Jane, with a gasp.

"He'll never be better; I'm 'feared he's gone, ma'am," answered the nurse, grimly, looking on his open mouth, and wiping away the claret from his chin.

"It can't be, my good Lord! it can't—quite well this minute—talking—why, it can't—it's only weakness, nurse! for God's sake, he's not—it is not—it can't be," almost screamed Lady Jane.

The nurse only nodded her head sternly, with her eyes still riveted on the face before her.

"He ought 'a bin let alone—the talkin's done it," said the woman in a savage undertone.

In fact she had her own notions about this handsome young person who had intruded herself into Sir Jekyl's sick-room. She knew Beatrix, and that this was not she, and she did not like or encourage the visitor, and was disposed to be sharp, rude, and high with her.

Lady Jane sat down, with her fingers to her temple, and the nurse thought she was on the point of fainting, and did not care.

Donica Gwynn entered, scared by a word and a look from Tomlinson as he passed her on the stair. She and the nurse, leaning over Sir Jekyl, whispered for a while, and the latter said—

"Quite easy—off like a child—all in a minute;" and she took Sir Jekyl's hand, the fingers of which were touching the table, and laid it gently beside him on the coverlet.

Donica Gwynn began to cry quietly, looking on the familiar face, thinking of presents of ribbons long ago, and school-boy days, and many small good-natured remembrances.

CHAPTER XXXVI.

In the Chaise.

Hearing steps approaching, Donica recollected herself, and said, locking the room door—

"Don't let them in for a minute."

"Who is she?" inquired the nurse, following Donica's glance.

"Lady Jane Lennox."

The woman looked at her with awe and a little involuntary courtesy, which Lady Jane did not see.

"A relation—a—a sort of a niece like of the poor master—a'most a daughter like, allays."

"Didn't know," whispered the woman, with another faint courtesy; "but she's better out o' this, don't you think, ma'am?"

"Drink a little wine, Miss Jennie, dear," said Donica, holding the glass to her lips. "Won't you, darling?"

She pushed it away gently, and got up, and looked at Sir Jekyl in silence.

"Come away, Miss Jennie, darling, come away, dear, there's people at the door. It's no place for you," said Donica, gently placing her hand under her arm, and drawing her toward the study door. "Come in here, for a minute, with old Donnie."

Lady Jane did go out unresisting, hurriedly, and weeping bitterly.

Old Donica glanced almost guiltily over her shoulder; the nurse was hastening to the outer door. "Say nothing of us," she whispered, and shut the study door.

"Come, Miss Jennie, darling; do as I tell you. They must not know."

They crossed the floor; at her touch the false door with its front of fraudulent books opened. They were now in a dark passage, lighted only by the reflection admitted through two or three narrow lights near the ceiling, concealed effectually on the outside.

The reader will understand that I am here describing the architectural arrangements, which I myself have seen and examined. At the farther end of this room, which is about twenty-three feet long, is a niche, in which stands a sort of cupboard. This swings upon hinges, secretly contrived, and you enter another chamber of about the same length. This room is almost as ill-lighted as the first, and was then stored with dusty old furniture, piled along both sides, the lumber of fifty years ago. From the side of this room a door opens upon the gallery, which door has been locked for half a century, and I believe could hardly be opened from without.

At the other end of this dismal room is a recess, in one side of which is fixed an open press, with shelves in it; and this unsuspected press revolves on hinges also, shutting with a concealed bolt, and is, in fact, a door admitting to the green chamber.

It is about five years since I explored, under the guidance of the architect employed to remove this part of the building, this mysterious suite of rooms; and knowing, as I fancied, thoroughly the geography of the house, I found myself with a shock of incredulity thus suddenly in the green chamber, which I fancied still far distant. Looking to my diary, in which I that day entered the figures copied from the ground plan of the house, I find a little column which explains how the distance from front to rear, amounting to one hundred and seventy-three feet, is disposed of.

Measuring from the western front of the house, with which the front of the Window dressing-room stands upon a level, that of the green chamber receding about twelve feet:—

	ft.	in.

Window dressing-room or hexagon	12	0
Green chamber	38	0
Recess	2	0
First dark room	23	0
Recess	1	6
Second dark room	23	0
Recess	1	6
Study	25	0
Wall	1	0
Sir Jekyl's bed-room	27	0
Ante-room	10	0
Stair, bow-window of which forms part of the eastern front	9	0
	—	—
	—	—
	—	—

173   0

I never spoke to anyone who had made the same exploration who was not as much surprised as I at the unexpected solution of a problem which seemed to have proposed bringing the front and rear of this ancient house, by a "devilish cantrip slight," a hundred feet at least nearer to one another than stone mason and foot-rule had ordained.

The rearward march from the Window dressing-room to the foot of the back stair, which ascends by the eastern wall of the house, hardly spares you a step of the full distance of one hundred and seventy-three feet, and thus impresses you with an idea of complete separation, which is enhanced by the remote ascent and descent. When you enter Sir Jekyl's room, you quite forget that its great window looking rearward is in reality nineteen feet nearer the front than the general line of the rear; and when you stand in that moderately proportioned room, his study, which appears to have no door but that which opens into his bed-room, you could not believe without the evidence of these figures, that there intervened but two rooms of three-and-twenty feet in length each, between you and that green chamber, whose bow-window ranks with the front of the house.

Now Lady Jane sat in that hated room once more, a room henceforward loathed and feared in memory, as if it had been the abode of an evil spirit. Here, gradually it seemed, opened upon her the direful vista of the future; and as happens in tales of magic mirrors, when she looked into it her spirit sank and she fainted.

When she recovered consciousness—the window open—eau de cologne, sal volatile, and all the rest around her, with cloaks about her knees, and a shawl over her shoulders, she sat and gazed in dark apathy on the floor for a time. It was the first time in her life she had experienced the supernatural panic of death.

Where was Jekyl now? All irrevocable! Nothing in this moment's state changeable for ever, and ever, and ever!

This gigantic and inflexible terror the human brain can hardly apprehend or endure; and, oh! when it concerns one for whom you would have almost died yourself!

"Where is he? How can I reach him, even with the tip of my finger, to convey that one drop of water for which he moans now and now, and through all futurity?" Vain your wild entreaties. Can the dumb earth answer, or the empty air hear you? As the roar of the wild beast dies in solitude, as the foam beats in vain the blind cold precipice, so everywhere apathy receives your frantic adjuration—no sign, no answer.

Now, when Donica returned and roused Lady Jane from her panic, she passed into a frantic state—the wildest self-upbraidings; things that made old Gwynn beat her lean hand in despair on the cover of her Bible.

As soon as this frenzy a little subsided, Donica laid her hand firmly on the young lady's arm.

"Come, Lady Jane, you must stop that," she said, sternly. "What *I* hear matters nothing, but there's others that must not. The house full o' servants; *think*, my darling, and don't let yourself *down*. Come away with me to Wardlock—this is no place any longer for you— and let your maid follow. Come along, Miss Jennie; come, darling. Come by the glass door, there is no one there, and the chaise waiting outside. Come, miss, you must not lower yourself before the like o' them that's about the house."

It was an accident; but this appeal did touch her pride.

"Well, Donnie, I will. It matters little who now knows everything. Wait one moment—my face. Give me a towel."

And with feminine precaution she hastily bathed her eyes and face, looking into the glass, and adjusted her hair.

"A thick veil, Donnie."

Old Gwynn adjusted it, and Lady Jane gathered in its folds in her hand; and behind this mask, with old Donnie near her, she glided down-stairs without encountering anyone, and entered the carriage, and lay back in one of its corners, leaving to Gwynn, who followed, to give the driver his directions.

When they had driven about a mile, Lady Jane became strangely excited.

"I must see him again—I *must* see him. Stop it. I *will*. Stop it." She was tugging at the window, which was stiff. "Stop him, Gwynn. Stop him, woman, and turn back."

"Don't, Miss Jennie; don't, darling. Ye could not, miss. Ye would not face all them strangers, ma'am."

"Face them! What do you mean? *Face* them! How dare they? I despise them—I *defy* them! What is their staring and whispering to me? I'll go back. I'll return. I *will* see him again."

"Well, Miss Jennie, where's the good? He's cold by this time."

"I must see him again, Donnie—I *must*."

"You'll only see what will frighten you. You never saw a corpse, miss."

"Oh! Donnie, Donnie, Donnie, don't—you mustn't. Oh! Donnie, yes, he's gone, he is—he's *gone*, Donnie, and *I*'ve been his ruin. I—I— my wicked, wretched vanity. He's gone, lost for ever, and it's *I* who've done it all. It's *I*, Donnie. I've destroyed him."

It was well that they were driving in a lonely place, over a rough way, and at a noisy pace, for in sheer distraction Lady Jane screamed these wild words of unavailing remorse.

"Ah! my dear," expostulated Donica Gwynn. "*You*, indeed! Put that nonsense out of your head. *I* know all about him, poor master Jekyl;

a wild poor fellow he was always. *You*, indeed! Ah! it's little you know."

Lady Jane was now crying bitterly into her handkerchief, held up to her face with both hands, and Donica was glad that her frantic fancy of returning had passed.

"Donnie," she sobbed at last—"Donnie, you must never leave me. Come with me everywhere."

"Better for you, ma'am, to stay with Lady Alice," replied old Donnie, with a slight shake of her head.

"I—I'd rather die. She always hated him, and hated me. I tell you, Gwynn, I'd swallow poison first," said Lady Jane, glaring and flushing fiercely.

"Odd ways, Miss Jane, but means kindly. We must a-bear with one another," said Gwynn.

"I hate her. She has brought this about, the dreadful old woman. Yes, she always hated me, and now she's happy, for she has ruined me— quite ruined—for nothing—all for nothing—the cruel, dreadful old woman. Oh, Gwynn, is it all true? My God! is it true, or am I mad?"

"Come, my lady, you must not take on so," said old Gwynn. "'Tisn't nothing, arter all, to talk so wild on. Doesn't matter here, shut up wi' me, where no one 'ears ye but old Gwynn, but ye must not talk at that gate before others, mind; there's no one talking o' ye yet—not a soul at Marlowe; no one knows nor guesses nothing, only you be ruled by me; you *know* right well they can't guess nothink; and you must not be a fool and put things in people's heads, d'ye *see*?"

Donica Gwynn spoke this peroration with a low, stern emphasis, holding the young lady's hand in hers, and looking rather grimly into her eyes.

This lecture of Donica's seemed to awaken her to reflection, and she looked for a while into her companion's face without speaking, then lowered her eyes and turned another way, and shook old Gwynn's hand, and pressed it, and held it still.

So they drove on for a good while in silence.

"Well, then, I don't care for one night—just one—and to-morrow I'll go, and you with me; we'll go to-morrow."

"But, my lady mistress, *she* won't like that, mayhap."

"Then *I*'ll go alone, that's all; for another night I'll not stay under her roof; and I think if I were like myself nothing could bring me there even for an hour; but I am not. I am quite worn out."

Here was another long silence, and before it was broken they were among the hedgerows of Wardlock; and the once familiar landscape was around her, and the old piers by the roadside, and the florid iron gate, and the quaint and staid old manor-house rose before her like the scenery of a sick dream.

The journey was over, and in a few minutes more she was sitting in her temporary room, leaning on her hand, and still cloaked and bonneted, appearing to look out upon the antique garden, with its overgrown standard pear and cherry trees, but, in truth, seeing nothing but the sharp face that had gazed so awfully into space that day from the pillow in Sir Jekyl's bed-room.

CHAPTER XXXVII.

Old Lady Alice talks with Guy.

As Varbarriere, followed by Doocey and Guy, entered the hall, they saw Dives cross hurriedly to the library and shut the door. Varbarriere followed and knocked. Dives, very pallid, opened it, and looked hesitatingly in his face for a moment, and then said—

"Come in, come in, pray, and shut the door. You'll be—you'll be shocked, sir. He's gone—gone. Poor Jekyl! It's a terrible thing. He's gone, sir, quite suddenly."

His puffy, bilious hand was on Varbarriere's arm with a shifting pressure, and Varbarriere made no answer, but looked in his face sternly and earnestly.

"There's that poor girl, you know—my niece. And—and all so unexpected. It's awful, sir."

"I'm very much shocked, sir. I had not an idea there was any danger. I thought him looking very far from actual danger. I'm *very* much shocked."

"And—and things a good deal at sixes and sevens, I'm afraid," said Dives—"law business, you know."

"Perhaps it would be well to detain Mr. Pelter, who is, I believe, still here," suggested Varbarriere.

"Yes, certainly; thank you," answered Dives, eagerly ringing the bell.

"And I've a chaise at the door," said Varbarriere, appropriating Guy's vehicle. "A melancholy parting, sir; but in circumstances so sad, the only kindness we can show is to withdraw the restraint of our presence, and to respect the sanctity of affliction."

With which little speech, in the artificial style which he had contracted in France, he made his solemn bow, and, for the last time for a good while, shook the Rev. Dives, now Sir Dives Marlowe, by the hand.

When our friend the butler entered, it was a comfort to see one countenance on which was no trace of flurry. *Nil admirari*—his manner was a philosophy, and the convivial undertaker had acquired a grave suavity of demeanour and countenance, which answered all occasions—imperturbable during the comic stories of an after-dinner sederunt—imperturbable now on hearing the other sort of story, known already, which the Rev. Dives Marlowe recounted, and offered, with a respectful inclination, his deferential but very short condolences.

Varbarriere in the meanwhile looked through the hall vestibule and from the steps, in vain, for his nephew! He encountered Jacques, however, but he had not seen Guy, which when Varbarriere, who was in one of his deep-seated fusses, heard, he made a few *sotto voce* ejaculations.

"Tell that fellow—he's in the stable-yard, I dare say—who drove Mr. Guy from Slowton, to bring his chaise round this moment; we shall return. If his horses want rest, they can have it in the town, Marlowe, close by; I shall send a carriage up for you; and you follow, with all our things, immediately for Slowton."

So Jacques departed, and Varbarriere did not care to go up-stairs to his room. He did not like meeting people; he did not like the chance of hearing Beatrix cry again; he wished to be away, and his temper was savage. He could have struck his nephew over the head with his cane for detaining him.

But Guy had been summoned elsewhere. As he walked listlessly before the house, a sudden knocking from the great window of Lady Mary's boudoir caused him to raise his eyes, and he saw the grim apparition of old Lady Alice beckoning to him. As he raised his hat, she nodded at him, pale, scowling like an evil genius, and beckoned him fiercely up with her crooked fingers.

Another bow, and he entered the house, ascended the great stair, and knocked at the door of the boudoir. Old Lady Alice's thin hand opened it. She nodded in the same inauspicious way, pointed to a seat, and shut the door before she spoke.

Then, he still standing, she took his hand, and said, in tones unexpectedly soft and fond—

"Well, dear, how have you been? It seems a long time, although it's really nothing. Quite well, I hope?"

Guy answered, and inquired according to usage; and the old lady said—

"Don't ask for me; never ask. I'm *never* well—always the same, dear, and I hate to think of myself. You've heard the dreadful intelligence—the frightful event. What *will* become of my poor niece? Everything in distraction. But Heaven's will be done. I shan't last long if this sort of thing is to continue—quite impossible. There—don't speak to me for a moment. I wanted to tell you, you must come to me; I have a great deal to say," she resumed, having smelt a little at her vinaigrette; "but not just now. I'm not equal to all this. You know how I've been tried and shattered."

Guy was too well accustomed to be more than politely alarmed by those preparations for swooning which Lady Alice occasionally saw fit to make; and in a little while she resumed—

"Sir Jekyl has been taken from us—he's gone—awfully suddenly. I wish he had had a little time for preparation. Ho, dear! *poor* Jekyl! Awful! But we all bow to the will of Providence. I fear there has been some dreadful mismanagement. I always said and knew that Pratt was a quack—positive infatuation. But there's no good in looking to secondary causes, Won't you sit down?"

Guy preferred standing. The hysterical ramblings of this selfish old woman did not weary or disgust him. Quite the contrary; he would have prolonged them. Was she not related to Beatrix, and did not this kindred soften, beautify, glorify that shrivelled relic of another generation, and make him listen to her in a second-hand fascination?

"You're to come to me—d'ye see?—but not immediately. There's a—there's some one there at present, and I possibly shan't be at home. I must remain with poor dear Beatrix a little. She'll probably go to Dartbroke, you know; yes, *that* would not be a bad plan, and I of course must consider her, poor thing. When you grow a little older you'll find you must often sacrifice yourself, my dear. I've served a long apprenticeship to that kind of thing. You must come to Wardlock, to my house; I have a great deal to say and tell you, and you can spend a week or so there very pleasantly. There are some pictures and books, and some walks, and everybody looks at the monuments in the church. There are two of them—the Chief Justice of Chester and Hugo de Redcliffe—in the "Gentleman's Magazine." I'll show it to you when you come, and you can have the carriage, provided you don't tire the horses; but you must come. I'm your kinswoman—I'm your relation—I've found it all out—very near—your poor dear father."

Here Lady Alice dried her eyes.

"Well, it's time enough. You see how shattered I am, and so pray don't urge me to talk any more just now. I'll write to you, perhaps, if I find myself able; and *you* write to *me*, mind, directly, and address to Wardlock Manor, Wardlock. Write it in your pocket-book or you'll forget it, and put "to be forwarded" on it. Old Donica will see to it. She's very careful, I *think*; and you promise you'll come?"

Guy did promise; so she said—

"Well, dear, till we meet, good-bye; *there*, God bless you, dear."

And she drew his hand toward her, and he felt the loose soft leather of her old cheek on his as she kissed him, and her dark old eyes looked for a moment in his, and then she dismissed him with—

"There, dear, I can't talk any more at present; there, farewell. God bless you."

Down through that changed, mysterious house, through which people now trod softly, and looked demure, and spoke little on stair or lobby, and that in whispers, went Guy Deverell, and glanced upward, involuntarily, as he descended, hoping that he might see the beloved shadow of Beatrix on the wall, or even the hem of her garment; but all was silent and empty, and in a few seconds more he was again in the chaise, sitting by old Varbarriere, who was taciturn and ill-tempered all the way to Slowton.

By that evening all the visitors but the Rev. Dives Marlowe and old Lady Alice, who remained with Beatrix, had taken flight. Even Pelter, after a brief consultation with Dives, had fled Londonwards, and the shadow and silence of the chamber of death stole out under the door and pervaded all the mansion.

That evening Lady Alice recovered sufficient strength to write a note to Lady Jane, telling her that in consequence of the death of Sir Jekyl, it became her duty to remain with her niece for the present at Marlowe. It superadded many religious reflections thereupon; and offering to her visitor at Wardlock the use of that asylum, and the society and attendance of Donica Gwynn, it concluded with many wholesome wishes for the spiritual improvement of Lady Jane Lennox.

Strangely enough, these did not produce the soothing and elevating effect that might have been expected; for when Lady Jane read the letter she tore it into strips and then into small squares, and stamped upon the fragments more like her fierce old self than she had appeared for the previous four-and-twenty hours.

"Come, Donica, you write to say I leave this to-morrow, and that you come with me. You said you'd wish it—you must not draw back. You would not desert me?"

I fancy her measures were not quite so precipitate, for some arrangements were indispensable before starting for a long sojourn on the Continent. Lady Jane remained at Wardlock, I believe, for more than a week; and Donica, who took matters more peaceably in her dry way, obtained, without a row, the permission of Lady Alice to accompany the forlorn young wife on her journey.

CHAPTER XXXVIII.

Something more of Lady Jane Lennox.

"See, Doctor Pratt—how do you do?—you've been up-stairs. I—I was anxious to see you—most anxious—this shocking, dreadful occurrence," said the Reverend Dives Marlowe, who waylaid the Doctor as he came down, and was now very pale, hurrying him into the library as he spoke, and shutting the door. "The nurse is gone, you know, and all quiet; and—and the quieter the better, because, you know, that poor girl Beatrix my niece, she has not a notion there was any hurt—a wound, you see, and knows nothing in fact. I'll go over and see that Slowton doctor—a—a gentleman. I forget his name. There's no need—I've considered it—none in the world—of a—a—that miserable ceremony, you know."

"I don't quite follow you, sir," observed Doctor Pratt, looking puzzled.

"I mean—I mean a—a coroner—that a——"

"Oh! I see—I—I see," answered Pratt.

"And I went up, poor fellow; there's no blood—nothing. It may have been apoplexy, or any natural cause, for anything I know."

"Internal hæmorrhage—an abrasion, probably, of one of the great vessels; and gave way, you see, in consequence of his over-exerting himself."

"Exactly; a blood-vessel has given way—I see," said the Reverend Dives; "internal hæmorrhage. I see, exactly; and I—I know that Slowton doctor won't speak any more than you, my dear Pratt, but I may as well see him, don't you think? And—and there's really no need for all that terrible misery of an inquest."

"Well, you know, it's not for me; the—the family would act naturally."

"The family! why, look at that poor girl, my niece, in hysterics! I would not stake that—that *hat* there, I protest, on her preserving her wits, if all that misery were to be gone through."

"Does Lady Alice know anything of it?"

"Lady Alice Redcliffe? Quite right, sir—very natural inquiry;—not a syllable. She's, you know, not a—a person to conceal things; but she knows and suspects nothing; and no one—that nurse, you told me, thought the hurt was an operation—not a soul suspects."

And thus the Reverend Dives agreed with himself that the scandal might be avoided; and thus it came to pass that the county paper, with a border of black round the paragraph, announced the death of Sir Jekyl Marlowe, Baronet, at the family residence of Marlowe Manor, in this county, the immediate cause of his death being the rupture of a blood-vessel in the lungs, attended by internal hæmorrhage. By the death of Sir Jekyl Marlowe, it further stated, "a seat in Parliament and a deputy lieutenancy for this county become vacant." Then came a graceful tribute to Sir Jekyl's value as a country gentleman, followed by the usual summary from the "Peerage," and the fact that, leaving no male issue, he would be succeeded in his title and the bulk of his estates by his brother, the Reverend Dives Marlowe.

So in due course this brother figured as the Reverend Sir Dives Marlowe, and became proprietor of Marlowe Manor, where, however, he does not reside, preferring his sacred vocation, and the chance of preferment—for he has grown, they say, very fond of money—to the worldly life and expensive liabilities of a country gentleman.

The Reverend Sir Dives Marlowe, Bart., is still unmarried. It is said, however, that he was twice pretty near making the harbour of matrimony. Lady Bateman, the relict of Sir Thomas, was his first object, and matters went on satisfactorily until the stage of business was arrived at; when unexpectedly the lovers on both sides were pulled up and thrown on their haunches by a clause in Sir Thomas's will, the spirit of which is contained in the Latin words, *durante viduitate*. Over this they pondered, recovered their senses, shook hands, and in the name of prudence parted good friends, which they still are.

The second was the beautiful and accomplished Miss D'Acre. In earlier days the Reverend Dives would not have dreamed of anything so imprudent. Time, however, which notoriously does so much for us, if he makes us sages in some particulars, in others, makes us spoonies. It is hard to say what might have happened if a more eligible bridegroom had not turned up in George St. George Lighton, of Seymour Park, Esq. So that Dives' love passages have led to nothing, and of late years he has attempted no further explorations in those intricate ways.

I may as well here mention all I know further about Lady Jane Lennox. I cannot say exactly how soon she left Wardlock, but she did not await Lady Alice's return, and, I think, has never met her since.

Sir Jekyl Marlowe's death was, I suppose, the cause of the abandonment of General Lennox's resolution to proceed for a divorce. He remained in England for fully four months after the Baronet's death, evidently awaiting any proceedings which the family might institute, in consequence, against him. Upon this point he was fiercely obstinate, and his respectable solicitor even fancied him "cracked." With as little *fracas* as possible, a separation was arranged—no difficult matter—for the General was open-handed, and the lady impatient only to be gone. It was a well-kept secret; the separation, of course, a scandal, but its exact cause enveloped in doubt. A desperate quarrel, it was known, had followed the General's return from town, but which of the younger gentlemen, then guests at Marlowe, was the hero of the suspicion, was variously conjectured. The evidence of sojourners in the house only deepened the mystery. Lady Jane had not shown the least liking for anyone there. It was thought by most to have a reference to those old London stories which had never been quite proved. A few even went the length of conjecturing that something had turned up about the old General, which had caused the explosion.

With an elderly female cousin, Donica Gwynn, and her maid, she went abroad, where she has continued nearly ever since, living rather solitarily, but not an outcast—a woman who had been talked about unpleasantly, but never convicted—perhaps quite blameless, and therefore by no means excluded.

But a secret sorrow always sat at her heart. The last look of that bad man, who, she believed, had loved her truly though guiltily—summoned as he talked with her—irrevocably gone. Where was he now? How was it with him?

"Oh, Jekyl! Jekyl! If I could only know if we are ever to meet again—forgiven!"

With fingers clasped together under her cloak, and eyes upturned to the stars in the beautiful Italian skies, she used, as she walked to and fro alone on the terrace of her villa, to murmur these agonised invocations. The heedless air received them; the silent stars shone cold above, inexorably bright. But Time, who dims the pictures, as well as heals the wounds of the past, spread his shadows and mildews over these ghastly images; and as her unselfish sorrow subsided, the sense of her irrevocable forfeiture threw its everlengthening shadow over her mind.

"I see how people think—some wonder at me, some accept me, some flatter me—all suspect me."

So thought she, with a sense of sometimes nearly insupportable loneliness, of resentment she could not express, and of restlessness—dissatisfied with the present, hopeless of the future. It was a life without an object, without a retrospect—no technical compromise, but somehow a fall—a fall in which she bitterly acquiesced, yet which she fiercely resented.

I don't know that her Bible has yet stood her in stead much. She has practised vagaries—Tractarian sometimes, and sometimes Methodist. But there is a yearning, I am sure, which will some day lead her to hope and serenity.

It is about a year since I saw the death of General Lennox in the "Times," an event which took place rather suddenly at Vichy. I am told that his will contains no allusion to Lady Jane. This, however, was to have been expected, for the deed of separation had amply provided for her; so now she is free. But I have lately heard from old Lady Alice, who keeps her memory and activity wonderfully, and maintains a correspondence with old Donnie Gwynn, that she shows no symptom of a disposition to avail herself of her liberty. I have lived long enough to be surprised at nothing, and therefore should not wonder if hereafter she should do so.

CHAPTER XXXIX.

The Last.

Old Lady Alice, who liked writing and reading letters, kept up an active correspondence with her grandson, and that dutiful young gentleman received them with an interest, and answered them with a punctuality that did him honour.

Shortly after Lady Jane Lennox's departure from Wardlock, Lady Alice Redcliffe and her fair young charge, Beatrix, arrived at that discreet old dower house. Old Lady Alice, who, when moved, could do a good-natured thing, pitying the solitariness of her pretty guest, so soon as she thought her spirits would bear it, invited first the Miss Radlowes, and afterwards the Miss Wynkletons—lively young ladies of Beatrix's time of life—who helped to make Wardlock less depressing. These hospitalities led to "invites;" and so the time passed over without the tedium that might have been looked for, until the period drew near when Beatrix was to make the Italian tour she had arranged with that respectable and by no means disagreeable family, the Fentons of Appleby. A rumour reached Guy that Drayton was to be one of the party. This certainly was not pleasant. He alluded to it in his next letter, but Lady Alice chose to pass the subject by.

There had been no step actually taken in the threatened lawsuit since the death of Sir Jekyl. But there were unpleasant rumours, and Pelter and Crowe were in communication with the Rev. Sir Dives Marlowe on the subject, and he occasionally communicated his peevish sense of poor Jekyl's unreasonableness in having died just when everything was at sixes and sevens, and the unfairness of his having all the trouble and so little of the estates.

Varbarriere, I suppose, was on good terms once more with his nephew. There was no more talk of Algeria, and they were now again in London. That corpulent old gentleman used to smile with an unctuous scorn over the long letters with which Lady Alice occasionally favoured him.

"My faith! she must suppose I have fine leisure, good eyes also, to read all that. I wish, Guy, she would distinguish only you with her correspondence. I suppose if I answer her never, she will cease some time."

He had a letter from her while in London, on which he discoursed in the above vein. I doubt that he ever read it through.

Guy received one by the same post, in the conclusion of which she said—

"Beatrix Marlowe goes in a few days, with the Fentons, to Paris, and thence to Italy. My house will then be a desert, and I miserably solitary, unless you and your uncle will come to me, as you long since promised, and as you well know there is nothing to prevent. I have written to him, naming Wednesday week. I shall then have rooms in which to place you, and you positively must not refuse."

Under this hospitable pressure, Varbarriere resolved to make the visit to Wardlock—a flying visit of a day and night—rather to hear what she might have to say than to enjoy the excellent lady's society. From Slowton, having there got rid of their railway dust and vapour, the gentlemen reached Wardlock at the approach of evening. In the hall they found old Lady Alice, her thin stooping figure cloaked and shawled for a walk, and her close bonnet shading her hollow and wrinkled face.

Hospitable in her way, and really glad to see her guests, was the crone. She would have dismantled and unbonneted, and called for luncheon, and would have led the way into the parlour; but they would not hear of such things, having refreshed at Slowton, and insisted instead on joining the old lady in her walk.

There is a tall glass door in the back hall, which opens on the shorn grass, and through it they passed into the circumscribed but pretty pleasure-ground, a quadrangle, of which the old house, overgrown with jessamine and woodbine, formed nearly one side; the opposite garden wall, overtopped with ancient fruit-trees, another; and screens of tall-stemmed birch and ash, and an underwood of juniper and evergreens, the others; beds of brilliant verbena here and there patterned the green sod; and the whole had an air so quaint and cloister-like, as drew forth some honest sentences of admiration from old Varbarriere.

They strolled among these flowers in this pleasant seclusion for a time, until Lady Alice pronounced herself fatigued, and sat down upon a rustic seat, with due ceremony of adjustment and assistance.

"Sit down by me, Mr. Strangways. Which am I to call you, by-the-bye?"

"Which you please, madam," answered Varbarriere, with the kind of smile he used with her—deferential, with, nevertheless, a suspicion of the scornful and amused in it, and as he spoke he was seated.

"As for you, grandson," she continued, "you had better take a walk in the garden—you'll find the door open;" she pointed with her parasol to the old-fashioned fluted door-case of Caen stone in the garden wall; "and I want to talk a little to my friend, M. de Varbarriere—Mr. Strangways, as I remember him." And turning to that sage, she said—

"You got my letter, and have well considered it, I trust?"

"I never fail to consider well anything that falls from Lady Alice Redcliffe."

"Well, sir, I must tell you——"

These were the last words that Guy heard as he departed, according to orders, to visit her ladyship's old-fashioned garden. Could a young fellow fancy a duller entertainment? Yet to Guy Deverell it was not dull. Everything he looked on here was beautified and saddened by the influence that had been there so recently and was gone.

Those same roses, whose leaves were dropping to the earth, she had seen but a day or two ago in their melancholy clusters; under these tall trees she had walked, here on this rustic seat she had rested; and Guy, like a reverent worshipper of relics, sat him down in the same seat, and, with a strange thrill, fancied he saw a pencilled word or two on the arm of it. But no, it was nothing, only the veining of the wood. Why do ladies use their pencils so much less than we men, and so seldom (those I mean whose relics are precious) trace a line by chance, and throw this bread upon the waters, where we poor devils pull cheerless against wind and tide?

Here were flowers, too, tied up on tall sticks. He wondered whether Beatrix ever tended these with her delicate fingers, and he rose and looked at the bass-mat with inexpressible feeling.

Then, on a sudden, he stopped by a little circle of annuals, overgrown, run into pod, all draggled, but in the centre a split stick and a piece of bleached paper folded and stuck across it. Had she written the name of the flower, which perhaps she sowed? and he plucked the stick from the earth, and with tender fingers unfolded the record. In a hideous scrawl, evidently the seedsman's, "Lupines" sprawled across the weather-beaten brown paper.

He raised his eyes with a sigh, and perceived that the respectable gardener, in a blue body-coat with brass buttons, was at hand, and eyed him with a rather stern inquisitiveness. Guy threw the stick down carelessly, feeling a little foolish, and walked on with more swagger than usual.

And now he had entered that distant part of the garden where dark and stately yew hedges, cut here and there in arches, form a meditative maze. With the melancholy yearnings of a lover he gazed on these, no doubt the recent haunts of that beautiful creature who was his day-dream. With a friendly feeling he looked on the dark wall of yew on either side; and from this solemn walk he turned into another, and—saw Beatrix!

More beautiful than ever he thought her—her features a little saddened. Each gazed on the other, as the old stories truly say in such cases, with changing colour. Each had imagined the other more than a hundred miles away. Neither had fancied a meeting likely, perhaps possible. The matter hung upon the wills of others, who might never consent until too late. A few days would see Beatrix on her way to Italy with the Fentons; and yet here were she and Guy Deverell, by the sleight of that not ill-natured witch, old Lady Alice, face to face.

I don't know exactly what Guy said. I don't know what she answered. The rhetoric was chiefly his; but he held her hand in his, and from time to time pleaded, not quite in vain, for a word from the goddess with glowing cheeks and downcast eyes, by whose side he walked. Low were those tones, and few those words, that answered his impetuous periods; yet there was a magic in them that made him prouder and more blessed than ever his hopes had dared to promise.

Sometimes they stopped, sometimes they walked slowly on, quite unconscious whether they moved or paused—whether the birds sang or were silent—of all things but their love—in a beautiful dream.

They had surprised one another, and now in turn both were surprised by others; for under one of those airy arches cut so sharply in the yew hedge, on a sudden, stood old Lady Alice and Monsieur Varbarriere—the Enchanter and the Fairy at the close of a tale.

Indulgently, benevolently, the superior powers looked on. The young people paused, abashed. A sharp little nod from Lady Alice told them they were understood. Varbarriere came forward, and took the young lady's hand very kindly, and held it very long, and at the close of his salutation, stooping towards her pretty ear, murmured something, smiling, which made her drop her eyes again.

"I think you both might have waited until I had spoken to you; however, it does not signify much. I don't expect to be of any great consequence, or in any great request henceforward."

Her grandson hastened to plead his excuses, which were received, I must allow, with a good grace.

In matters of true love, I have observed, where not only Cupid applauds, but Plutus smiles, Hymen seldom makes much pother about his share in the business. Beatrix did *not* make that tour with the Fentons. They, on the contrary, delayed their departure for rather more than a month; and I find Miss Fenton and Miss Arabella Fenton among the bridesmaids. Drayton did not attend the wedding, and oddly enough, was married only about three weeks after to Lady Justina Flynston, who was not pretty, and had but little money; and they say he has turned out rather cross, and hates the French and all their products, as "utter rot."

Varbarriere has established two great silk-factories, and lives in France, where they say gold pours in upon him in streams before which the last editor of "Aladdin" and Mr. Kightley of the "Ancient Mythology" hang their heads. His chief "object" is the eldest son of the happy union which we have seen celebrated a few lines back. They would have called the boy Herbert, but Varbarriere would not hear of anything but Guy. They say that he is a prodigy of beauty and cleverness. Of course, we hear accounts of infant phenomena with allowance. All I can say is, "If he's not handsome it's very odd, and he has at least as good a right to be clever as most boys going." And as in these pages we have heard something of a father, a son, and a grandson, each bearing the same name, I think I can't do better than call this tale after them—GUY DEVERELL.

THE END.

PRINTING OFFICE OF THE PUBLISHER.

Im The Story

personalised classic books

UNIQUE GIFT

FOR KIDS, PARTNERS AND FRIENDS

Timeless books such as:

Alice in Wonderland · The Jungle Book · The Wonderful Wizard of Oz
Peter and Wendy · Robin Hood · The Prince and The Pauper
The Railway Children · Treasure Island · A Christmas Carol

Romeo and Juliet · Dracula

Highly Customizable · **Change** Books Title · **Replace** Characters Names with yours · **Upload** Photo for inside pages · **Add** Inscriptions

Visit
Im The Story .com
and order yours today!

Lightning Source UK Ltd.
Milton Keynes UK
UKOW05f2208060617

302843UK00020B/1662/P